What the reviewers are saying about

Happiness Is Still Home Made

"This book is practical, easy to read and to remember. His manner of presentation and openness of discussion will free up some of the tensions which make the family the most maligned unit of society today."

—Augsburg Reading Club

"This is a warm and friendly book. It will do you and your family good."

—Atlanta Journal

"This book is loaded with anecdotes that illustrate the author's points. *Happiness Is Still Home Made* will serve as the focal point for group discussions as well as for individual readers."

—Santa Cruz Sentinel

"The author emphasizes that the Christian home is the citadel of strength through strain and test, through life and death. It builds for eternity. Laymen as well as ministers will find helpful instruction in this book. It is also a very appropriate gift book."

—The Ministry

"Here is a lively little book for people interested in making marriage satisfying and rewarding, and in making home Christian and creative. Ranging from courtship to old age there is something here for every member of the family."

—Brandenton Herald

"This is an excellent book. It deals in a new way about a subject that is familiar to all. This is easy and fast reading. A profitable reading experience awaits that husband and wife who will read and discuss this book together."

—*Choice Books* magazine

HAPPINESS IS STILL

HOME MADE

by T. Cecil Myers

A Key-Word Book

Word Book, Publishers

Waco, Texas

Grateful acknowledgment is made to the National Council of the Churches of Christ in the United States of America for permission to quote from the Revised Standard Version of the Bible, Copyright © 1946, 1952, © 1971, 1973.

ISBN 0–87680–830–5
Library of Congress Catalog Card Number 73–85827.

Printed in the United States of America.
First Printing—June 1969
Second Printing—November 1970
Third Printing—July 1972

First Word Paperback Printing—April 1973
First Key-Word Edition—October 1976

Contents

Introduction

The family is having a hard time, but despite the rise in divorce rates, the unhappiness in homes that remain together, scandals here and there, there is an increasing interest in the family. I would like to think that more and more of us are realizing that a good family is the nation's greatest asset. Bishop Hazen G. Werner, who has been an inspiration to me in the field of the family, has said, "Like Greenwich time, the family is the deciding unit of existence." Hopefully we are beginning to see this.

This book is for those interested in making marriage satisfying and rewarding—in making home Christian and creative. Much of the material has been given in family life consultations and institutes. The scope of these chapters ranges from courtship to "old age." There is something for every member of the family. The making of a good home begins at birth and lasts a lifetime, and requires love, patience, a sense of humor, understanding, faith in God and in man. A lifetime of determined effort in family living assures us that "at evening time it shall be light!"

My sincere appreciation to Mrs. Joe R. Colley for careful preparation of the manuscript.

To

William Thomas Myers and Charles Judson Myers, our sons, whose love is a constant source of inspiration.

1

▰▰▰▰▰▰▰▰

Happiness Is Still Home Made

*For this cause shall a man leave his father and mother,
and cleave to his wife; And they twain shall be one
flesh; so then they are no more twain, but one flesh.*
Mark 10:7, 8

Henry W. Grady, one of the south's most distinguished
statesmen, loved the city of Washington. The buildings
intrigued him, the important people impressed him, the
beautiful parks were an inspiration to him. He frequently
said that Washington was the heartbeat of American culture.

Once when Mr. Grady was on his way home to Georgia,
he stopped to spend the night at a simple farm home
in Virginia. He received the usual welcome given a noted
traveler. The family was glad to have him, for he brought
news of the world and something to talk about for days.

After supper, the entire family went to the "parlor"
and the father got the Bible and read from it. All present
knelt for prayer. The old man prayed for everyone he
could think of: family members present and absent, politicians, teachers, preachers, statesmen, heads of state over
the world. When the prayer was finished, the mother
went to the kitchen to finish up, the children soon went

11

to bed, and Henry Grady and the father talked awhile. When the household was settled for the night, Mr. Grady said he lay thinking a long time. Washington was not really the heartbeat of American culture. Simple homes like this one, where the Bible is read and prayer is made, where there is mutual respect for one another, and the basic principles of the Christian faith are practiced—here is the heartbeat of our nation. Later Henry Grady said, "The home is the mudsill of our American civilization!"

Around us, all is change. "Change and decay in all around I see . . ." the hymn writer declares. The bulldozer might well be the symbol of the American city. Fashions come and go. The hemline rises and falls. Last year's cars give way to the new. Medicine prescribed six months ago may be obsolete now. Everything is in a state of change, but the family survives change. Forms of the family may change, and there may be deviations from the established patterns; but over the centuries, men have returned again and again to the family unit as the highest form of fulfillment for the human race. This is why there is a feeling of nostalgia when we hear the strains of, "Be it ever so humble, there's no place like home!"

James W. Clarke told of an experience during World War I. After days of marching and savage fighting in the trenches, the men retired to a rest area. While they were there, Sir Harry Lauder came to entertain them. Dressed in full Highland costume, he climbed on a kitchen table and sang such songs as "Roaming in the Gloaming," "Just a Wee Doech and Doris," "I Love a Lassie." He was about to step down, when out of the immortal 51st Scottish Division came a voice with real anguish in it: "Harry! Harry! For God's sake sing us 'The Wee Hoose Among The Heather'." That was not just a cry from one lonely heart, but a cry that rises from the heart of the human race.

No wonder William E. Hocking said, "Where there are no families, there can be no state!" Someone else has called home "the nuclear germinal cell from which comes the dynamic that shapes history." The family is the nucleus of civilization. Robert Ingersoll regarded "marriage as the holiest institution among men. Without the family relation, there is no life worth living; without the family fireside, there is no human advancement." Whether you live in a hut in the hollow or a mansion on the hill, a one room efficiency or a ten room penthouse, your home is earth's most important place. Your home is "First Church" no matter where it is. Nothing can take its place or substitute for its importance. Everybody knows this— politicians know and try to create the image of a family man; advertisers slant their pitch toward the family. Schools organize PTA's to get the family involved. Churches institute family life programs to include all the family.

The family is the deciding factor in our existence.

Home is the polar point of civilization around which all else revolves. Edward R. Gibbon suggested that one cause for the fall of the Roman Empire was the alarming increase in divorce and the breaking up of the Roman home. When home is strong and vital, schools, churches, and government will be strong and vigorous. But when the homes of any community are riddled with immorality, lack discipline, evidence no real love, depend on material values alone, fail to teach respect for people, then there is little that schools and churches and government can do. No nation has ever been able to survive the breakdown of the family. Nations survive military defeat, depression, famine, flood, fire, governmental changes, but when homes break down, so do schools, churches, government, and everything else that is worthwhile.

More homes break up in the United States each year

than in any other country. For every four marriages performed, at least one ends in divorce. And the experts insist that the gap between the number of marriages and the number of divorces is getting narrower each year.

Home is the beginning point of everything. Here life makes up its mind. It is not just the beginning place of biological life, but of moral, ethical, mental, spiritual, and emotional life as well. Parents have the very first chance to affect the feelings, the beliefs, the ideas of the child. Someone has wisely said that parents have done at least half of all they can do for their child by the time he is six! The home fulfills many functions, but there are three primary ones: it provides sustenance for children and teaches them the essential art of self-preservation; it provides the first lessons in social living; it gives an education in fundamental values.

Tragically, not only does good begin at home, so does evil in far too many instances. For example, I was visiting several years ago, and stopped to call on a widow and her teen-age daughter. While we were visiting, the telephone rang. The mother said, "Honey, answer the telephone, and tell whoever it is that I'm not at home.". . . A survey made among some college students asked about drinking. For those who admitted that they drank, there was a further question, "Where did you learn to drink?" Seventy-five percent wrote that they learned to drink at home with father and mother. . . . A little boy took five dollars from his mother's purse. His father had him on the carpet. The boy finally broke into an angry tirade, "Daddy, why are you mad because I took five dollars from mama's pocketbook? I heard you tell mama last night after we went to bed that you beat the government out of fifteen hundred dollars on your income tax as slick as a whistle." *Home is where life makes up its mind.*

You see, home is where youth are prepared for the path of life. A prominent judge once said, "We adults spend far too much time preparing the path for our youth and far too little time preparing our youth for the path!" Most of the preparation for the path must take place in the family, or it likely does not take place!

Home is where respect for law and order is learned. What happens to a child's sense of value when he sees his daddy run a red light just because no policeman is in sight, or who brags about fishing all season without a license without getting caught? When a family sits around the table and hears father and mother disparage the mayor, the governor, the president, and belittle teachers, policemen, and others in authority, what happens to respect for law and order? It is no wonder that teachers in school cannot control children. A teacher told me recently, "We try to teach the children good manners in the cafeteria, but they insist on eating like their parents anyway!" And they insist on acting like their parents, and putting into practice what their parents have said in their attitude toward law and order and authority. Gordon H. Schroeder tells of a mother and her eight-year-old son peering through the fence at famous Fort Ticonderoga. Suddenly the mother said, "Son, I believe that hole under the fence is large enough for you to crawl through and see the fort without paying." I suspect when the guard at the gate turned his head a little boy scrambled under the fence, and a mother thought they got away with it. And maybe later the same boy, not so little now, scrambled through a skylight to enter a store or went through an open window in an apartment to ransack a house. Law and order must be taught. They must be taught at home, or they may not be learned.

Respect for persons is learned at home. Bishop Hazen G. Werner comments, "The taproot of reality in the Christian family is the recognition of the sacred meaning of each person in that intimate relationship." Living together at home teaches respect for persons. It is here that we learn that human personality is the most sacred thing on earth, and that each person has dignity and worth because "God formed man . . . and breathed into his nostrils the breath of life; and man became a living soul" (Genesis 2:7). Man is God's highest creation, and anything that fetters or denies or destroys human personality is a gross sin. If children learn this at home, they can move into the wider world and have respect for all people as the children of one Father and brothers one of another.

Our present broken human relationships, especially between the races, is mute testimony to the fact that we have done a poor job at home in teaching that all men are made in the image of God, and the accident of color does not lessen that divinity. Children usually have no race prejudice until it is taught. But when they hear "nigger" and "wop" and "dago" and "kraut" and "whitey" at home, questions rise in their impressionable minds, and pretty soon comes the conviction that one race is better than another. "My daddy says so!" It doesn't matter much what the church says about brotherhood—and the church has said and done too little—unless church people in their homes teach respect for persons of all kinds and all places as children of a loving heavenly Father. John C. Wynn commented, "What difference does it make which Bible stories we tell them at bedtime if they see us living daily as if we had never opened the dust covered Book?" Our words and actions teach them everything about how we feel about people!

At home, children learn the real meaning of love. In a society where love and lust are confused and where the word *love* expresses our feelings toward everything from chocolates to the family dog to God, we must help children understand the real meaning of love. William E. Hocking said in *The Coming World Civilization*, "For the family is the most direct embodiment of human love; and human love is, in its own complete self-consciousness, inseparable from the love of God. It is the natural context for a sacrament, inasmuch as it is by way of human love that the divine is most frequently and concretely discovered." [1] Love must be seen as self-giving, not self-seeking. It must be learned in terms of friendship, brotherhood, a genuine desire for the best for the object of one's affection. When this is true, there is respect for the body of another person, his mind, his emotions. There is only the desire to make another happy and give oneself in service to God and man. Love is all of one piece: Love of mother and child; love of husbands and wives; love for friends, sweethearts, God! It is found in the giving of oneself to a task, in the earnest effort to lift the level of mankind's living. For as Anders Nygren has said, "To see without loving is to stare into darkness!" In my counseling with families over nearly a quarter of a century, one truth stands out most clearly: the need for love. All people need love, and all people want love. It is on the basis of love that the ills of the world and the family will be solved. Jesus said, "Thou shalt love the Lord thy God . . . thy neighbor . . . thyself!" Life comes alive and takes on meaning when we learn to love in the highest sense. Smiley Blanton wrote, "For without love, we lose the will to live. Our mental and physical vitality is impaired, our resistance is lowered, and we succumb to illnesses that often prove fatal. We may escape actual death, but what remains is a meager and barren existence, emotionally so impoverished that we can only be called half alive." [2] The family is where love is learned.

Horace Bushnell said, "Home and religion are kindred

---

[1] William Ernest Hocking, *The Coming World Civilization* (New York: Harper and Brothers, 1956), p. 130.

[2] Smiley Blanton, *Love or Perish* (New York: Simon and Schuster, 1956), p. 4.

words, home because it is the seat of religion; religion because it is the sacred element of home . . . A house without a roof would scarcely be a more indifferent home than a family without religion." Religion is not something a child gets in Sunday school. It begins in the family or it doesn't begin. Unless a child learns to love Christ, read the Bible, and pray in the family, it is highly unlikely that he will learn it at all. Years ago, a little boy named Tommy was in a membership class in our church. We talked about what it means to be a Christian and what is involved in being a member of the church. Tommy wanted to become a Christian and join the church with the other boys and girls. His parents were members of the church, but they seldom attended Sunday school or worship. Tommy did most of his going alone, while daddy spent Sunday in undershirt and ragged pants sitting in the shade reading the comics or tinkering with an old car or fooling with his dogs. When the class was over, Tommy went home and told his mother what he wanted to do. She was indignant and called to put me in my place for influencing her boy to join the church. "I want him to make up his own mind." No words of mine could change her. We went through the same procedure the next year, and then a third time a year later. After the third try, Tommy dropped gradually out of any church activity. To my knowledge, he has never been back to Sunday school or church. He has a family of his own now, and neither he nor they are interested in the church in any way.

Religion begins at home, and no matter how carefully the church works with children, unless there is coopera-tion and encouragement in the home, the whole thing is pretty hopeless. Parents ought to influence their children for Christ and the church. Certain movies influence them for drinking and illicit sex. Many comic books influence them for all kinds of mad and impossible schemes. Some television programs teach violence and bitterness. Playmates exert influence over them for a multitude of things. Parents had better try positively to influence them for religion and faith and membership in a church.

No intelligent gardener leaves anything to chance. He doesn't let the tomatoes or jimson weed, onions or crab grass, dahlias or bitter weed make up their own mind. I see gardeners influencing their gardens every day. Why not treat our children with at least as much regard as our gardens? Religion begins at home. That makes home very important. Martin Luther once said, "The home is the God-ordained place for training in Christian character."

Happiness is still home made. There is no substitute for it. Home is important beyond our wildest imagination. Bishop Hazen G. Werner, in his book, *Christian Family Living* has this marvelous paragraph: "Here in the family the deepest experiences take place. Home is where things happen that matter most, where life hides its real crises. Here familiarity breeds contempt or contentment. Here, too, you bring your wounds from out of a world of competitive living for healing. Here is where you lay bare your depletions of body and soul. Young and old come home like clocks run down to be wound up again. Here you expose your emotional weaknesses, that through understanding you are led to find reason and courage to change. Here, too, is expressed the impassioned hunger to belong. Here character and inner depths of being are nourished by spiritual renewal. All this goes on by divine help. It cannot be otherwise." [3]

[3] Hazen G. Werner, *Christian Family Living* (Nashville: Abingdon, 1959), p. 18.

2

♦♦♦♦♦♦♦♦

Little Foxes Do
Spoil The Vines!

Take us the foxes, the little foxes, That spoil the vineyards; For our vineyards are in blossom. Song of Solomon 2:15.

In New England there lived an old couple named Si and Mirandy. Their lives on the farm had been hard. They were getting quite old and both were nearly deaf and their eyesight was failing. Si had never been much of a lover, and during all the years he had never told Mirandy that he loved her. One night they were sitting in the parlor. Si was reading the farm paper and Mirandy was crocheting. The old man kept looking across the table, thinking of all the things his wife had done for him over the years: the biscuits she had baked, the socks she had mended, cows milked, children borne. It was almost more than he could do to keep from taking her in his arms and telling her he loved her, but he managed to control himself for a while. Suddenly, he jumped to his feet and looked her straight in the face and shouted, "I'm proud of you, Mirandy!" She fixed him with an icy stare and replied, "I'm tired of you too, Si!"

No one can deny the fact that there are problems in our homes. Anyone who works day after day in a pastoral or counseling relationship is painfully aware of much that is wrong. The statistics are startling enough. The last year for which figures are available, there were 1,527,000 marriages, and 395,000 divorces. But figures are not very revealing. Many couples stay together and suffer torment, rather than risk public opinion, or for economic reasons, or even for the children's sake, when all the time they would rather be divorced.

The rapid rise in the crime rate indicates that something is wrong at home. When people get the kind of start they need in life, feel loved and wanted, stable and secure, they are more apt to adjust to a changing society without criminal deviations. The rise in the rate of youth problems to the point where three million young people come into conflict with the law each year points up the size of the problem in the family. I talked recently with a pretty little girl who styled herself a "hippie." She wasn't really. She just hadn't combed her hair or had a bath in several days. Inside she was just a frightened little girl who still needed her mother and daddy but didn't want to admit it. When we talked, she kept insisting that nobody understood. Her mother and daddy wouldn't let her live her own life. She wanted freedom. Her parents had made some mistakes, and I'm sure they didn't understand her completely, but who doesn't make mistakes and who does understand completely? But a telephone call to a little town not far from Atlanta resulted in a tearful reunion, and a little girl going home to parents who said they'd try if she would.

There is a strange statement in Song of Solomon for which the scholars have no adequate explanation. "Take us the foxes, the little foxes, That spoil the vineyards; For our vineyards are in blossom." They think this may refer to some ancient fertility rite. But set down as it is in this love song in the Old Testament, it is suggestive for our purpose. The little foxes may have destroyed the vineyards. They certainly do destroy the family. Little things burrow in: wrong attitudes, unreasonable demands, an uncompromising spirit, wrong values, selfish goals. These little foxes destroy the sanctity of the home and bring all that we had hoped and longed for crashing about our ears. Let's look at some of these little foxes. What is wrong in our homes?

A changing concept of marriage. Far too many people approach it with an "à la carte" attitude, take it or leave it—if it doesn't work out, we can get out. A young man said to his minister, "We have no illusions; we know how uncertain marriage is these days; and we are not interested in buying a house, or furniture, or getting ourselves involved in any way. We own a car, and we think that is about all we need in view of the temporariness of marriage."

We have forgotten the words in the marriage ritual, ". . . so long as you both shall live" and ". . . till death do us part." Often it runs like this: "till we disagree on something" or ". . . till she crosses me." A young woman came recently to talk about getting married. She said she was twenty years old. I asked if she had been married previously. She replied, "Oh yes, twice, and I have the divorce papers to prove it." Unfortunately, there is no longer any stigma attached to the multiple married person. The changing concept of marriage presents problems in the family. Children of such multiple married people suffer in many ways. But they grow up feeling that marriage is temporary.

Dr. J. Randolph Ray observes, "Living together is hazardous enough without the added handicap of 'merchandise returnable.' "[1]

---

[1] J. Randolph Ray, *My Little Church Around the Corner* (New York: Simon and Schuster, 1957), pp. 216, 217.

Home values have come to mean cash values. Frequently we see signs that read, "HOME FOR SALE." You can't buy a home. You can buy a house, or you can buy lumber and brick and mortar and glass and furniture and build a house. A home is something that must be grown. It is interesting to watch a couple get ready for marriage. They search high and low for a suitable place to live, the exact china and silver pattern, the precise kind of furniture to fit their tastes. They must have a stereo with the same delicate sound as the one that was playing when he proposed. The car must be nearly new, though not nearly paid for. There must be all the comforts of home. Yet, when it comes to counseling for marriage, preparation for the essential matters in marriage, there isn't time. Believe me, there is a vast difference between home values and cash values. Money is important—it may not be everything but it is so far ahead of whatever is in second place that there is no contest. At least that is our attitude in the family, and this is one of the little foxes that destroy. So we slave and drive and both partners work in order to have "things"—when "things" never guarantee happiness at home. Our impatience to acquire possessions in a hurry is a social disease. I am convinced that a mark of maturity is to be able to postpone the immediate for the ultimate.

Too many fathers don't "tote their end of the log" in making home what it ought to be. This is a tough world for fathers and husbands. Many of them leave early Monday morning, travel all week, and return Friday night or Saturday with tired bodies and aching minds. It isn't easy to fulfill the role of father under these conditions. An interesting survey was made among seventh and eighth grade boys over a two-week period to discover how much time they spent with their fathers. Three hundred boys kept an accurate record. Most of the boys saw their fathers only at the dinner table—a number never saw their fathers for days at a time, some not even for weeks. The average time that father and son had alone together for an entire week was seven and one-half minutes.[2]

Somewhere in the Old Testament are the words, "Take the boy to his mother," and from then until now a lot of fathers have left discipline, moral, ethical, spiritual training to the mother. "I don't want to be bothered with family problems when I get home at night," commented a father recently. But just as father cooperated in bringing the child into the world, so he must cooperate in the moral, ethical, spiritual training of the child.

Too many women have lost sight of the sacredness of their calling as wives, mothers, and homemakers. Dr. Peter Marshall preached a sermon entitled, "Keepers of the Springs"—that is precisely what women are. It seems to me that we have made a mistake in our entire educational procedure. We prepare women for everything in the world except the important role of homemaking, and fail completely to glamourize this most vital of all roles. No wonder a woman that is trained to be an executive secretary or a teacher is bored stiff with cleaning house, or shopping for groceries, or tending a baby.

I believe there are some false elements associated with the emancipation of womanhood. We favor equality for womanhood, and the Christian church has worked to bring this about. More often than not, however, equality has been interpreted as the right of women to take on the vices of men. While this is certainly their right, it would be so much better in terms of permanent values for women to lift the standard for men. We have always felt that women were made of a little finer clay than men, and that somehow they ought to lift men to new heights of morality and spiritual achievement. A woman's highest

---

[2] Gordon H. Schroeder—*Christian Herald*, Literature Department, 1701 James St., Syracuse 6, New York.

calling still is that of motherhood. This is the most creative task to which she may devote her talents. Nothing
is of greater importance, and nothing has more lasting
glamour than the rearing of children that are honorable,
righteous, God-fearing, and useful. We remember Susan-
nah Wesley principally because of two of her children:
John and Charles. We know Mrs. Lincoln because of her
Abe. The highest reward that can come to any woman
is that of children that turn out well.

The enormous complexities of our world have done
something to home. And the multiplication of gadgets
has driven us apart instead of drawing us together. How
long has it been since your family has been really together
for an evening? When we get up in the mornings, daddy
goes his way and the children scatter to school, grandma
goes one way, and grandpa goes another. Often we don't
even see each other for days. Some wag has done a
parody on "Home Sweet Home" that goes:

> Home sweet home, the poet sang
> In days that were of old.
> But now the home has just become
> A parking place, I'm told.
> We park to eat a bite, to sleep,
> And then we're on the run;
> The office, movies, clubs, and dates,
> No time for family fun.

Then there is the influence of television, movies, comic
books, magazines, and radio on the family. While all of
these have contributed something good to our lives as
families, they have had a definite influence in changing
the moral tone of the family and of our nation. Drinking
is accepted in most movies and is advertised on almost
all media without any stigma attached to it, but the
liquor forces never show the end result of alcoholism.
People who have been married several times are often

the stars of the movies and television shows and are featured in magazine stories. Sex in its rawest forms can be seen and read about by all ages. Violence is a major part of the entertainment presented for the American audience, ranging from the western to the sophisticated police drama. What ought to be the mightiest force on earth for education in morals and good living frequently becomes the medium by which immorality is made to seem acceptable. *This is not so little a fox.*

All the gadgets and comforts we enjoy have done something to the spirit of the family. There was a time when the family worked as a unit to produce all its supplies. Now this is done outside the home, and there are few things of a creative nature for the children and parents to do together. Dishwashers rob mothers and daughters of the opportunity for "girl talk" over the dishpan. A yard man at the apartment mows the lawn, depriving the father and son of a chance to be together. Heat comes from a distant boiler room, and so there is no fire to make. It is true that we all enjoy these comforts, but in a way they have robbed us of a togetherness that nothing else has provided. So we go to the YMCA, or the club, or depend on the school, or to a lesser degree, the church, for activities for the family. And these are very often segregated so that the whole family is rarely together for entertainment, or worship, or study. This "separateness" is a little fox that destroys the family.

Still another little fox that affects us deeply is the fact that we move so often. We are a mobile society—a nation on wheels. This is understandable, since big companies transfer their executives so often, and men move from one place to another looking for better opportunities. I have had the experience of electing men to the Official Board in the church, only to have them transferred before they could be installed. One pastor told me recently that in a given year, one-third of his Official Board was moved.

While this makes us a cosmopolitan nation, it does something to our sense of stability. What must junior feel when he is transferred in the middle of the school year? Once may be all right, but I'm thinking of a junior to whom this happened four times in six years of high school.

We all need roots—the sense of belonging somewhere and of being a part of some community. My only nostalgia over being a Methodist minister is at this point. Some people I know have lived in the same town since birth and have developed a feeling of security and friendship that a man on the move can never know. I have been among the more fortunate ministers, having served only four churches in my ministry. Our mobility takes us away from grandparents and our relatives, and we move to places where no one knows us. Sometimes this may be good, but it does something to the idea of family solidarity. Here is another little fox that eats at the family.

But perhaps all of these problems in the family are predicated on this last one: we have divorced home and religion. Religion and the family belong together, but we have separated them. Here are two simple illustrations. I had thirty-five boys and girls in a membership training class one year. Toward the end of the period, I asked if any of them had never heard father or mother pray or ask a blessing. Twenty-one of the thirty-five lifted their hands to say they had never heard either parent pray . . . A lovely little girl quit coming to Sunday school, and I went to see why. Her mother said, "Preacher, little Janie has so much to do. She takes dancing and piano lessons, is active in her club at school and has her activities at the country club. Janie just had to give up something, so we decided she must give up Sunday school." What the writer of Deuteronomy predicted has come true: "Beware that thou forget not the Lord thy God . . . Lest when thou hast eaten and art full, and hast built goodly houses, and dwelt therein; and when thy herds and thy flocks multiply, and thy silver and thy gold is multiplied, and all that thou hast is multiplied; Then thine heart be lifted up, and thou forget the Lord thy God, which brought thee forth . . ." (8:11–20). This is the main reason families are in trouble today—they have forgotten God, and the many other problems confronting the American family are merely suggestive. But, I believe there are answers. Let's consider a few things we can do.

For one thing, say to yourself over and over, "My family, my home is the most important institution in the world!" Believe that fact. You'll probably not realize just how precious home is until you begin to get older, and one by one the family members scatter, and begin to die, and there comes a feeling of being left alone, without kindred to care. How important home is to sustain us! It fulfills our deepest needs for love and understanding, gives us emotional stability, and teaches us to live with people. How wonderful to be able to turn home at night as a retreat from the crises of the noisy business world and know that love is waiting. Here is where life's hurts are healed. Here new strength is found for the road. Here power is gained to move out to make a creative contribution for the day. Yes, home is wonderful. Maybe this is the reason nothing has ever been able to quite destroy it, though many forces have tried.

In the second place, we must see that the true values in life, and especially in the home, are not material but spiritual. It doesn't really matter how much money a family has, or how many comforts, unless there is love. A woman said recently, "My husband thinks all he has to do is bring home the bacon." He thought all that was necessary to make a home was money or things. Color television, modern freezers, a large bank account have no power to heal broken hearts or supply power for crises. Admiral Richard E. Byrd said: "At the end only two things really matter to a man, regardless of who he is; and they are the affection and understanding of his family . . . I realize how wrong my sense of values had been, and how I had failed to see that the simple, homely, unpretentious things of life are the most important." [3] When did he say these words? When he was in the Antarctic, alone, not sure that he would ever see family or home again. Lasting values at home are spiritual, personal, emotional, and not necessarily material.

In the third place, we must recover family feeling, that sense of unity that gives strength when all else would destroy. This is the feeling that makes us support each other when the going is tough. It is demonstrated in a father whose son was wayward, and caused the father much sorrow. One day another father said to him, "If he were my boy, I'd let him go!" The broken-hearted father replied, "If he were your boy, so would I, but he's my boy, and I can't let him down." Someone asked a thirteen year old boy, "What do you think makes a happy family?" He replied, "A happy family reminds me of a baseball team, with mom pitching, dad catching, the kids fielding, and with everyone taking turns at bat." This is family feeling.

In the fourth place, there must be some moral standards in the home by which the family lives. This permissive generation offers little direction and guidance. Children want standards. A young woman said to me recently, "I wish just once my mother would tell me this is what I must do." We are too inclined to live by situation ethics, doing what is expedient for a given situation. But there are some absolutes: The Ten Commandments, the Beatitudes, the Golden Rule, the dignity of personality. A judge said some time ago that he could solve the

---

[3] Lillian Eichler Watson, *Light From Many Lamps* (New York: Simon and Schuster, 1951), p. 250.

problem of juvenile delinquency with nine words: "Put daddy back at the head of the house." He did not mean set up a dictatorship. He simply meant that there must be some authority, some place where the buck stops, and can't be passed any more. By agreement, by understanding, every home ought to establish some minimum rules to govern conduct based on some absolutes that have withstood the test of centuries.

Fifth, home ought to be as attractive as possible. This does not require wealth. Soap, water, elbow grease, and imagination are the essential ingredients. Home ought to be so attractive that daddy can't wait to get there at night, and children never hesitate to invite their friends home with them. I sat across from a lovely sixteen-year-old one day. She was pregnant. We talked about the problem for awhile and then I asked, "Betty, do you ever bring your friends home on a date?" I could see her lips curl into a snarl, and she fairly spat out the words, "I wouldn't bring anybody to my house. The living room blinds are always closed, and the house smells bad. Once when I did take a friend home, daddy came padding through the living room barefooted and without a shirt. And they never would let us have any privacy. No, I never did take them home, and I never will!" I could understand her predicament.

Sixth, keep good literature handy, and especially the Bible. Psychologists tell us that we wake up thinking about what was on our minds when we went to sleep. Imagine! Think what our children must dream about after an evening of horror comics and television. I always look to see what a family reads. It is amazing to find *True Romance,* wild west weeklies, and movie magazines on the coffee table, and often not a sign of anything really fit to read. A Bible ought to be readily available for every person to read just before sleep. And the home library should be well stocked with a good variety of fine books and magazines that uplift—that leave out the smutty side of sex and portray decency, truth, and honor.

Finally, we must recover religion. Lewis Mumford said ". . . the family is the first area of our national life in which a swift renewal of faith, and act, and deed must take place." [4] Religion ought to be a vital part of every family. It ought to be as natural to talk of Jesus, prayer, church, faith as to talk of baseball and swimming. There should be a time set aside for worship with the entire family, where the Bible and other devotional classics are read, and where prayer is made, with all members of the family participating. Church attendance as a family unit ought to be as normal as breathing. Dr. Albert Schweitzer wrote in his *Memoirs of Childhood and Youth:* "From the service in which I joined as a child, I have taken with me into life a feeling for what is solemn, and a need for quiet and self-recollection without which I cannot realize the meaning of my life. I cannot, therefore, support the opinion of those who would not let the children take part in grown up people's services until they to some extent understand them. The important thing is not that they shall understand but that they shall feel something of what is serious and solemn. The fact that the child sees his parents full of devotion and has to feel something of devotion himself, that is what gives the service its meaning to him." [5] Should we insist on our children going to Sunday school and church? Yes, and we should insist on going with them. Will Durant, whom none would call an orthodox Christian, insists that infidelity in marriage is increasing because God has become little more than a

---

[4] Lewis Mumford, *Faith for Living* (New York: Harcourt, Brace and Company, 1940).

[5] Albert Schweitzer, *Dr. Albert Schweitzer's Memoirs of Childhood and Youth* (New York: The Macmillan Company, 1931), p. 62.

popular superstition in modern life. If the family is to stand, there must be a recovery of family religion. Ralph Pinelli, one time umpire in the National League, said, "I believe that even more important than a college education is the good, solid, practical religious training in the home and in the church. My mother taught me a proper scale of values, and trained me to live up to them."

In one of Mark Twain's stories, he has Adam standing by the grave of Eve. His mind wanders back over their years together: the Garden of Eden with its beauty and its bounteous supply of all good things; their willful sin, followed by their expulsion from the Garden; the birth of their sons, and later the murder of Abel by Cain; their years of hard labor to earn their bread by the sweat of their brow. Then Adam's mind comes back to the matter at hand, and he thinks of Eve and all that she meant to him, and he summed up the glory of home and family in six words: "Where she was, there was Eden." [6]

---

[6] Mark Twain: Quoted by Bishop Hazen G. Werner in sermon delivered at National Convention on Family Life, Chicago, October 19, 1962.

3

꙰꙰꙰꙰꙰꙰꙰꙰

Successful Marriage Is
Like A Three-Legged Stool!

What therefore God hath joined together, let not man put asunder. Mark 10:9

Forasmuch as John and Mary have consented together in holy wedlock, and have witnessed the same before God and this company, and thereto have pledged their faith each to the other and have declared the same by joining hands and by giving and receiving rings; I pronounce that they are husband and wife together, in the name of the Father, and of the Son, and of the Holy Spirit. Those whom God hath joined together let not man put asunder. Amen.

These words, in one form or another, are spoken nearly two million times in the United States each year. Couples will leave the altar with the bright sun of hope shining in their faces to launch new homes. Everytime I perform a wedding, I recall the words of the writer of Proverbs: "There be three things which are too wonderful for me, yea, four which I know not: The way of an eagle in the air; the way of a serpent upon a rock; the way of a ship in the midst of the sea; and the way of a man with a maid" (30:18–19). God made us this way, for each

35

other, that we may fulfill each other and complement each other in many ways. Monogamous marriage (some wag changed the word to monotonous)—one man, one woman—is God's way. He set us apart to live in families, and over the centuries this arrangement has proven the best.

Tragically, about one-fourth of the nearly two million marriages will end in failure. One woman said to me recently, "My marriage isn't a failure. It is a total disaster. I know now that it should never have been!" And in the course of our conversation, it came out that the minister-counselor had said to her and her groom-to-be that they ought to wait awhile before getting married anyway. Now, ashamed to go back to the minister who had tried to help them prepare, she seeks a way to salvage some of the pieces.

Seeing that homes are in jeopardy everywhere, we need to remind ourselves that marriages are not made in heaven, nor is a marriage consummated just because someone pronounced them husband and wife. Marriages begin way back in the preparation period, are blessed at the altar of the church, and then worked out in the lives of two people who are prepared for the experience, who love each other, and who take God with them into the new venture. Actually, too many marriages fail before they begin officially.

Stricter divorce laws are not the answer, though I am convinced that uniform divorce laws, uniform laws regulating child support, uniform regulations concerning legal separation across the country would help solve many a knotty problem. But the real guarantee for happier, better homes lies in a keener understanding of the meaning of marriage, better preparation for it, a determination to make it work, a willingness to share completely, and a vital religious faith. This means that in the home, the school, and the church better preparation must be made by the introduction of simple study courses on marriage, a sane attitude toward sex, and on human relations.

The young people of America are fortunate beyond measure. In some countries marriages are arranged by matchmakers, or parents work out a convenient arrangement between two families, often at the birth of babies. In many other lands, young people dare not marry across class lines, race lines, or out of their social group. But here, young people choose their friends, their dates, and ultimately their mates. The only restrictions placed on them are those given by the young person's own conscience, his own moral code, his religion, his training at home and in school. A closer relationship between parents and their young people, and between pastors and young people will create a more receptive mood for guidance and direction. But the final freedom to choose is theirs. This is a sacred freedom and ought to be used wisely and well.

One of the happiest times in life is that period we call courtship. It begins at varying times, usually about fourteen with group dating, followed by the separation into couples, and going steady by the senior high school year. Many young people think they must be married soon after high school, but one of the major causes of trouble in marriage comes from marrying too young. Sociologists suggest that the best ages for marriage are about twenty-one or twenty-two for the woman and twenty-two or twenty-three for the man. This gives time for maturity in every way. The fact of physical maturity is no guarantee of happiness in marriage. It takes some emotional, some mental, some spiritual maturity as well. Many a young woman has wailed to me, "Oh, if I had only waited until after college!" Or, "If I hadn't been in such a hurry. I hardly knew any other boys!" That is a part of the tragedy. Courtship is a time to make many friends. It does not mean that a young person is fickle, and runs from one boy to another, one girl to another, but it does mean that there is a variation in the dating experience, giving opportunity to be a little more certain of the type that is to be "the one and only." Each date is preparation for marriage, though it may not be seen this way. Each friendship is preparation for marriage, and the more friendships, the more nearly one is ready for marriage. Some poet put it well: "I love you, not only for what you are, but for what I am when I am with you!" That is what many friendships ought to do for us: bring out the best and develop it.

Courtship is the time to learn to distinguish between love and infatuation. A boy said to his father one night, "Dad, how will I know when the right girl for me comes along?" "Don't worry, son," replied Dad. "She'll tell you!" Infatuation is selfish, wants to get for itself. In infatuation, we "fall in love over and over again." Love is the opposite. Love is unselfish, giving, sharing, outgoing. We may be infatuated this week with the football captain, two months later with the basketball captain, and two months later with the baseball captain. There is a selfish note in each of these: look at me, see who my dates are. But authentic love is very different—Paul says it beautifully: "Love is not puffed up . . . seeketh not her own . . . never fails" (I Corinthians 13).

Courtship is no time to exploit sex. No greater fallacy exists than the one that says we must experiment with sex to see if we are compatible. Doctors tell us that almost any man and woman can be compatible, or can become compatible over the years. This fallacy becomes an excuse for license. I still believe, even in a time when reports tell us that many people have already had intercourse when they come to marriage, that a clean, pure body is the best gift a girl can bring her intended husband when they stand at the altar. There is no double standard. The same applies to the man. One of the loveliest things I have ever heard came in a counseling session with a couple. We had been talking about sex and the physical relationships in marriage. The bride-to-be, a beautiful girl, said softly, "Dr. Myers, I want you to know that I'm saving myself for him!" She said it without shame, or apology, and not as if she had missed something. Many marriages would end better if they started on a footing of mutual respect and brought the gift of purity to the altar.

Courtship is the time to decide what kind of mate you want, what characteristics he should have, what ideals he must hold. This is the time to set up some standards for marriage. An unknown poet said:

> At sweet 16, I first began
> To ask the good Lord for a man;
> At 17, I recall,
> I wanted someone strong and tall.
> The Christmas I reached 18,
> I fancied someone blond and lean.
> And then at 19 I was sure
> I'd fall for someone more mature.
> At 20, I thought I'd find
> Romance with someone with a mind.
> I retrogressed at 21
> And found college boys most fun.
> My viewpoint changed at 22,
> When 'one man only' was my cue.
> I broke my heart at 23
> And asked for someone kind to me.
> Then begged at blasé 24
> For anyone who wouldn't bore;
> Now Lord, that I'm 25
> Just send me someone who's alive!

Courtship is the time to learn to get along with people, to strengthen one's moral and spiritual foundations, to make some decisions that endure. I know some couples that begin every date with prayer. Silly? Maybe to some sophisticated people, but not silly to those seriously seeking to come to marriage prepared, and who want a marriage that will endure and be creative and rewarding. If two people cannot get along without constant quarreling and endless bickering on dates, why expect their marriage would be any different? And girls, don't ever marry a man with the idea that you will reform him later. If there are bad habits that ought to be broken, attitudes that ought to be changed, take care of these before marriage and then wait long enough to be sure they have been taken care of.

In short, courtship is the most important time of life. It is the time of preparation for marriage. Thus, it ought to be regarded with a sense of sacredness and awe. "Whether you wind up with a nest egg or a goose egg depends on the kind of chicken you marry."

Successful marriage is like a three-legged stool. All three legs are necessary to make it stand. So there are three ingredients that must go into marriage to insure its success.

The first is preparation. That is what we have been discussing. Everything that goes on in our lives from birth to marriage is preparation for marriage. Parents ought to realize this fact. The attitude of father and mother toward their marriage sets a pattern for the children. If there is always bickering and fighting in the family it will result in a reaction expressed to me by a pretty teenager, "If that's all there is to marriage, I want none of it!" If children never see father and mother kiss or show affection in other ways, they may become cold and unaffectionate toward the opposite sex. If the parents are cynical about the sacredness of marriage, children may develop a light attitude toward it. But if children see absolute loyalty of parents to each other, even in the little things; if they see affection expressed; if marriage is reasonably smooth with a minimum of quarreling; then children are most likely to develop positive attitudes toward marriage and family. This is not to say that father and mother won't have differences of opinion. A man who says that he and his wife have never had a cross word will lie about everything else. Someone asked an old man how he could be so healthy, have such a beautiful tan, and be so robust at his age. The old man replied, "When my wife and I married, we agreed that if one of us started an argument the other would go out in the yard. Well, I've spent much of my life in the yard!" Everything that goes on in the family is preparation for marriage and sets the stage for the kind of marriage our children will have.

But once the decision to marry has been made, another kind of preparation is essential. I will not marry a couple without a period of time set aside for counseling, usually lasting several hours and divided into several sessions dealing with a wide variety of subjects. It seems to me that the time spent in these sessions is most helpful and productive for the prospective bride and groom. In addition I always insist that couples consult with a competent physician. It is amazing that couples will spend much time in selecting a china pattern, a silver pattern, a place to live, furnishings for the home, and then think all they need do is show up for the ceremony at the set time and all is well. Many times, after counseling sessions, I have suggested that couples wait or that they not marry at all. Some have listened, some have not. Preparation is essential.

A young nurse came to my office one day and announced that she and a young doctor were to be married and wanted to know if I would perform the ceremony. I knew them both and said I would after we spent some time together in counseling. She said, "Now preacher, we don't need that stuff. We are both grown, we know the facts of life, we are both in the medical field and all we want is to get married." I said, "Jane, how did you become a nurse?

Did you just walk into the hospital and take a handful of hypodermic needles and start down the hall giving shots?" (And I promise you, the way some of them give shots, it seems that's what they did!) She looked startled, and replied, "No, I enrolled, and went to classes for months before they would even let me on the floor with patients! Then gradually, I did tasks for the patients, beginning with the bed pan brigade, and now I'm about to graduate!" Then I said, "Which do you think is more important: learning to be a good nurse or learning to be a good marriage partner?" "I see what you mean," she replied. "Set the dates and we'll be here." Marriage is one of life's three major choices, and adequate preparation that includes an understanding of the meaning of marriage and a philosophy to live by is absolutely essential.

The second leg of the stool is this: be sure it is love. You say, "Well, isn't that why everybody gets married?" Hardly. Some marry for convenience, some for economic reasons, some for companionship, and some because they must. The real foundation stone of a happy marriage is love that is genuine. Much of what we call love is nothing more than physical attraction. It means, "I love me and I want you." It is true that the physical aspect is important in love and marriage, and our first attraction for each other is often physical. But this is love in the kindergarten stage. Love includes mind and spirit as well. It implies understanding and respect. It desires only the best for its object. Love wants to give rather than get. Love finds happiness in making one's partner happy. It is an earnest and unbreakable good will. There is nothing selfish about it. The very best description of it is found in St. Paul's "Hymn to Love" (I Corinthians 13). Because of love, we can carry the daily load of work, the irritations of child care, the failures and successes of the average day. Love keeps us kindly. It never rejoices in the hurts and failures of others, but it rejoices in success. Love is that spiritual oneness that binds two lives, in every detail, inseparably together for time and eternity. Love does not end at death. It never fails.

Elizabeth Barrett Browning described love in the magnificent poem entitled "Sonnets from the Portugese," which she dedicated to her husband:

> How do I love thee? Let me count the ways.
> I love thee to the depth and breadth and height
> My soul can reach, when feeling out of sight
> For the ends of being and ideal Grace.
> I love thee to the level of everyday's
> Most quiet need, by sun and candle-light.
> I love thee freely, as men strive for Right;
> I love thee purely, as they turn from Praise.
> I love thee with the passion put to use
> In my old griefs, and with my childhood's faith.
> I love thee with a love I seemed to lose
> With my lost saints,—I love thee with the breath,
> Smiles, tears, of all my life!—and, if God choose,
> I shall but love thee better after death.

The third leg of the stool is: take God into marriage. I enjoy reading the marriage quizzes in popular magazines. Jane Goodsell brought laughter when she said: "My marriage doesn't even qualify as a failure. It's a disaster. But I didn't know it until I became addicted to those 'Are you happily married?' quizzes" (*American Weekly*, April 2, 1961). Most of them never mention religion as a necessary ingredient for making a happy marriage. In my counseling sessions with couples, I spend time on this area. The Psalmist listed four very ordinary human pursuits which cannot end successfully if God is left out: the building of houses, the life of the city, common labor, and the having of a family! One of the best known verses in the Psalms is, "Except the Lord build the house, they labor in vain that build it" (127:1). The wise man is not just concerned with the construction of dwellings; he is more concerned with the families that live in them. Many people set out on one of life's noblest ventures without really counting the cost. They "fall in love," get married, have children, and often run into difficulty.

The Psalmist has a contribution to make to the subject. He tells us that we have no right to expect success if we reduce marriage to a civil contract, the begetting of children to natural instincts, and the making of homes to chance. We must start with this: "Lo, sons are a heritage from the Lord, the fruit of the womb a reward." [1] Religion is the great preventer of home failure. For twenty-five years, I have offered the Christian faith as a cure for problems, and problems of the family are no exception. Two hearts knit together by a common faith in God need not fear circumstances. Sickness, poverty, adversity may come, but marriage based on the Christian faith stands. By religion I do not mean just church membership, though this is part of it. I mean rather the kind of faith that comes when two people are committed to Christ, to follow him, live by his teachings, receive his power. This is what it means to be a Christian. And this ought to be discussed during courtship. It is a paradox that we are embarrassed to talk about a matter as personal as one's faith, but we talk of sex with no embarrassment at all. If one is a Christian and the other not, what a privilege to introduce the non-Christian to Christ, then join the same church. There is value in belonging to the same church, standing together to sing the hymns of faith, praying the prayers of dedication and hope together, working together for the accomplishment of God's will and purposes in his world. Marriage is not a civil ceremony; it is a holy, sacred, religious thing, ordained by God and regulated by the state.

---

[1] *Interpreter's Bible*, Vol. 4 (New York, Nashville: Abingdon Press, 1955), p. 669.

I urge all couples to be married in the church. When the minister takes the hand of the bride from the father, places it in the hand of the groom, and has the groom say, "I, John, take thee Mary," in reality, it is the church giving Mary to John in the holiest of relationships. The same is true when the hand of the groom is laid in the hand of the bride and she repeats her vows.

Following the wedding, make religion practical and vital in the family. Talk of Jesus and God and prayer and salvation as unashamedly as bread and soap and the car. Set aside ten or fifteen minutes daily for devotions—Bible reading, prayer, and the reading of selections from the great spiritual classics. Use *The Upper Room*, or whatever devotional help your denomination provides. Keep this time inviolate as to time and place. The very atmosphere of the family ought to be that of faith and hope and love. Someone has said, "We may not always be as prepared as we should be; the lamp of love may flicker and almost go out at times; understanding may flee out the window; but if we love God, nothing can ultimately destroy the home!"

How will it all turn out? That depends on whether you are really ready, whether you love each other, and whether you take God with you. If you do, then in the words of Zechariah, spoken centuries before Jesus, ". . . at evening time it shall be light" (14:7).

4

To Keep Moonlight And Roses From Becoming Daylight And Dishes!

Frequently, I hear the greeting-question, "How is everything at home?" It may be just a casual greeting, but it merits serious consideration. If replies to the question were tabulated from all over the United States, we would have a disquieting answer on our hands, for everything is not all right in many of our homes. In the early days of America, there was about one divorce in five hundred marriages. By 1812 the average had risen to one in one hundred and ten. Recent figures show the ratio to be about one in four, and the prediction is that in a few years the ratio will be one divorce for two marriages. That is gloomy, and yet, I am optimistic about marriage. Many marriages are duels, but many more are real duets. More marriages succeed than fail. We have just celebrated our twenty-fifth wedding anniversary, and I can testify that marriage gets better and better. I didn't say easier and easier. But it is more fun as the years come and go than it was during the struggling years at the beginning. Sure, it is a gamble, but it is the kind of gambling that a minister can heartily recommend.

It is important that we ask and answer the question, "How is everything at home?" The home is the cradle for mankind. All of us begin there and most of us will end there. It is in the home that the heart dwells more than anywhere else, and no matter how humble or poor, the sentiments of John Howard Payne's song will apply: "Be it ever so humble, there's no place like home." Or at least that's the way it ought to be, and can be, if we make it so! It is in the home that we learn the lessons that form the core of existence for us: give and take, restraints that make for wholeness in life, respect for truth and honor, regard for the person and rights of other people. In the home, life hides its crises from the staring eyes of an unsympathetic public and offers balm for the harassed spirit. Tragically, we often save our worst selves for home. One writer said, "Private character is often public character turned wrong side out."

It is extremely important that we learn to keep romance in marriage if home is to be the place God meant it to be from the beginning, and if it is to carry us in the direction of the highest fulfillment of personality. Several years ago a young woman came to see me. She opened the interview by saying, "I have been married only a short time, but I have a question. Why can't married people continue to be sweethearts? For some reason, when you get married, courtship seems to stop. The sweet nothings you whispered to each other before marriage become nothing. You begin almost at once to take each other for granted." Successful marriage cannot be built upon the same kind of romance you knew before marriage. No couple could stand that! It was a sort of rosy "cloud nine." It was a burning sensation you couldn't quite locate. It was a rainbow path, a moonlit sheen on life. Let's face it, the kind of romance that successful marriage is built on does not cast a rosy glow around life, obscuring the

problems from our gaze and shutting out all reality—
except in the ads and fiction.

But, there is a romance appropriate for every age and
stage, and it is vital that we keep romance in marriage
if it is to succeed and if we are to achieve happiness for
ourselves and our children. We must take real care, lest
"moonlight and roses" become "daylight and dishes"! A
movie star has been quoted as saying that "marriage kills
romance." That ought not be and is not true if romance is
understood rightly. Someone has defined romance as "a
long story of love." The dictionary defines it as "a dreamy
imaginative habit of mind tending to dwell on the pic-
turesquely unusual." Both of these definitions are realis-
tically true! Romance in marriage is to be found in the
long story of love that began before marriage and found
fulfillment after marriage. It is to be found in the wonder
of relationships that are colorful, thrilling, and practical.
The romance of marriage includes all the joys of marriage
as well as the hazards. It is a way of life for a couple
within the bounds of responsible marriage.

We have a mistaken idea about happiness and romance
in marriage. Many of the marriage polls are made by
people who do not understand the deeper meaning of
marriage. In fact, I believe that some of them have been
prepared by people who have never been married. Happiness in marriage is not the result of having things, or even
of doing things. It is the result of being something, first
and foremost! Someone has defined a happy marriage as "a
continuing opportunity for a man and a woman to create
for themselves a new life separate and distinct and yet
inseparable from their individual lives—a life that can renew, challenge, and comfort them, that creates a real
home for them and their children." If this is a true definition, a happy marriage depends on the goals a couple has
in mind when they marry. To marry for money, or to sat-

isfy sexual desires, or for companionship, or for convenience is not goal enough for successful marriage. The highest goal is found in the Gospel of Mark, in words as old as the human race: "And they twain shall be one flesh; so then they are no more twain, but one flesh"—meaning that marriage is a union of love encompassing all of life: physical, spiritual, emotional, intellectual, and all.

We must then consider the matter of keeping romance in marriage in the light of the ultimate goal. Strangely enough, most of the problems that confront us in marriage are small ones. They seem trivial when isolated, but when continued from day to day, they build up into a disaster. Too many divorces are predicated on the little things that could have been ironed out easily in the beginning. A man walked across the United States backward. He was asked what gave him the most trouble. Was it getting across the Mississippi? The Rockies? No, neither of these. It was the sand in his shoes! We can handle the big crises when they come, but the little things throw us into a tailspin. We fall in love, marry, and assume the job is done. We seem to think that a marriage works out automatically. Nothing could be farther from the truth. Storms arise. Difficulties come. Dr. Louis H. Evans quotes a couple as saying, "If during our stormy matrimonial voyage, we do come to occasional patches of calm sea, we cannot enjoy them; we are so seasick from the other experiences." [1]

No, successful marriage doesn't just happen. It is worked out between two people, in spite of difficulties, through the little things and the big. Happy marriage is not an accomplishment. It is a journey. It is my self in relationship to another person. Plato used the ladder as an illustration. The two uprights represent two people who are in love and each rung represents something which draws

---

[1] Louis H. Evans, *Your Marriage: Duel or Duet?* (Westwood, N.J.: Fleming H. Revell, 1962), p. 12.

them together and holds them. From the lowest rung, physical attraction, to the highest, pure love for God, the two are bound in inseparable comradeship. The unity of the ladder must be maintained, for every rung is related to every other rung, and all the experiences, great and small, are important in making marriage happy.

All of us would like to keep romance in marriage. It can be done if we understand that what we *keep* is mostly what we create as we go along and not just something that happened to us sometime in the past. Marriage cannot live on what was. If we are successful in the general run of ordinary day-to-day living, and if we can make marriage a long story of love, filled with enough reassurance to balance the anxiety, enough gladness to dissipate the gloom, enough excitement to thrill and counteract the drudgery and boredom, the adventure of marriage will be the romance.

Here are some suggestions for keeping romance in marriage.

1. Go on courting and developing the love on which your marriage was founded. Love must deepen and mature. It is something that does not just come naturally. One man told me he didn't see any sense in chasing the bus after he'd already caught it. He wonders why his marriage isn't happy. That man has a lot to learn about love-making.

One of the problems involved at this point is flirtation. Many people have trouble forgetting the ones who got away. They spend precious time thinking about them or trying to make other conquests to prove that they are still desirable. Love must be constant and concentrated. You may not have gotten the best possible deal, but you got him (or her). It must have been a wife who first commented that husbands are of three classes: prizes, surprises, and consolation prizes. Much of the counseling that

I do deals with flirtations and triangle affairs. How much happier our marriages would be if we could realize that monogamous marriage means that we concentrate our attentions on the one to whom we are married. If we gave as much attention to making that one happy as some give to flirtations and other affairs, marriage would be happy.

2. Continue the little courtesies after marriage that were practiced before marriage. Remember? You wouldn't let her pick up a handkerchief. Now she can move the piano for all you care. You used to open the car door for her. Now, let her get in the best way she can. A rather large woman was struggling to get on the street car. Her husband watched, making no effort to help. She turned to him with blazing eyes and said, "John, you aren't as gallant as you were when you were a boy!" And John responded, "No, and you aren't as buoyant as you were when you were a gal, either."

It seems to me that an important prerequisite to this involves trying to look your best at home. Far too many of us take little pride in how we look in the privacy of home. Sure, home is a man's castle, and that is all the more reason for not looking like a bum in it. Remember how much time you spent primping and dressing for that date before you got married? Remember the trips to the barber shop and the shine parlor? Keeping is no less important than winning. A little boy was watching his mother make up her face for bed. Finally, he asked her what she was doing. She replied, "I'm making myself beautiful, son." He watched while she put on a heavy layer of cream and then wiped it off. "Humph! Didn't work did it!" was his only comment. A bit extreme, possibly, nevertheless, a little attention to this important detail may insure continued romance.

3. Learn to show appreciation. Dr. Norman Vincent Peale tells this story that every counselor could duplicate over and over.

A young woman, obviously in great mental distress, came to consult me. She was seriously considering leaving her husband, she said.

From her story it soon developed that all she needed was a little ordinary appreciation. Some more profound authority might call it affection but to me it seemed simpler than that.

I talked to the husband who said, "Oh, she would never leave me."

"Don't be so sure of that," I said.

He looked stunned. "Why, she could not do that. What could I ever do without her?"

"Did you ever tell her that you couldn't do without her?" I asked.

"Why, no," he answered, "I don't like that kind of talk and besides she knows it anyway."

"She may know it, but she wants to have it told to her just the same."

"Why?" he said.

"Don't ask me why," I replied. "That is just the way of women." (But it isn't only women; all of us have the deep craving to be appreciated which William James spoke about.)

"Have you by any chance brought her flowers or candy lately?"

He was a huge, clumsy looking fellow.

"Now, wouldn't I look fine lugging home flowers? I would look like a fool, me carrying flowers," he snorted.

"Just the same," I replied, "my professional prescription in this situation is to invest in some flowers and tell her you cannot get along without her." [2]

4. Learn self-control. Some wise man told a newly married couple to be sure and not both get mad at the same time. Fighting, shouting, pouting do not contribute to romance. Isn't it a pity that when our bodies grow up

---

[2] Norman Vincent Peale, *A Guide To Confident Living* (New York: Prentice-Hall, Inc., 1948), p. 189.

we don't always learn to act like grown-ups? Democracy ought to work better at home than anywhere else on earth. Two people old enough to get married ought to be mature enough to work out their differences in quiet tones, objectively, and then live with the decision best for them both and for their marriage. A lack of maturity causes about as many problems as anything I know. Sometimes in counseling, I act more like a referee than a counselor. Just because we have grown up physically is no sign that we have matured in other ways. This is a strong argument against teen-age marriages. Successful marriage also requires some maturity emotionally, spiritually, intellectually. Mary Dickerson Bangham has a poem she calls "Growing." She tells of a mother measuring the height of her daughter, when suddenly the daughter asked, "Mother, do you still grow?"

> I let the measuring rod drop.
> Do I still grow?
> This afternoon I suffered
> From unkind words,
> And yet I smiled.
> Last year I would have been proud,
> To make sharp reply.
> Yes child, I think so . . .
> But how hard and slow growing is!

We ought to determine that each day, in our marriage especially, we will grow up some to the maturity available to each of us.

5. Faith in each other is essential. The green-eyed monster has sent more people to divorce courts than almost anything else. Jealousy is a great enemy of marriage happiness. But, to have the trust of our marriage partner, each must be trustworthy. We must avoid doing the little things that might create suspicion and doubt about our loyalty and love.

6. Being together is an important ingredient in keeping romance in marriage. A woman said she couldn't understand where her husband went every night. So one night, she stayed home, and there he was! Togetherness in marriage is essential. The great word is sharing. If we are going to stay together, we must stay together and find and cultivate ways of enjoying each other's company.

7. Live every day as if it would be the last you would be together. If you knew that twenty-four hours from this minute one of you would die, how would you spend your last day together? Would you fight and quarrel? Jockey for position as head of the house? Insist on your own way? Maybe right here lies the practical application of what Jesus meant: "Treat other people exactly as you would like to be treated by them—this is the essence of all true religion" (Matthew 7:12, J. B. Phillips).[3]

8. Develop a lively faith in God and practice religion together. I grew up on the farm. Wagon wheels were a part of my boyhood. Did you ever examine one? The steel rim covers a wooden one around the outside. At the center is the hub. Running from rim to hub are the spokes. The closer the spokes get to the hub, the closer they get to each other. So in the family. The closer two people get to God—the hub of all life—the closer they get to each other. The poet put it well:

> Live not without thy God;
> However low or high
> In every home should be
> A window to the sky.

It may be a cliché, but nothing better has come along: "Families that pray together, stay together!" At least, they have a better chance of it than those who don't. Put

[3] J. B. Phillips, *The New Testament in Modern English* (New York: The Macmillan Company, 1958).

in a conspicuous place in your home these words and read them several times a day: "Except the Lord build the house, they labor in vain that build it."

I remember hearing a story when I was a boy about a farmer who had a large pond in his pasture from which the cattle drank. A strange sort of weed began to grow in the bottom of the pond, and before long it had taken over completely. The fish died, and the water was not good for the cattle. The farmer drained the pond and dug out the weeds, but they came back. The county agent suggested several kinds of chemicals. These were tried without success. The farmer was about to give up when someone suggested that he try setting willow trees around the edge of the water. He was skeptical, but willing to try anything. To his surprise, as the willows grew, the weeds began to die. The explanation was simple. The willows sent their roots deep into the soil under the bed of the pond, took out the plant food, and starved the weeds. Soon, the water was clear and good again. This story illustrates better than I can say what happens when we plant in our homes love and consideration and patience and understanding and prayer and God. There is no room for the ugly when the good and true and lovely fill everything.

5

❦❦❦❦❦❦❦❦

Five Commandments

For Modern Parents

Who is the greatest in the kingdom of heaven? And Jesus called a little child unto him . . . Matthew 18:1, 2.

Several years ago, I was at home in Chickamauga, Georgia, for a few days vacation. My stepfather was an invalid, having suffered a severe stroke at the age of sixty-four. He was on the bed constantly. One afternoon, my mother asked me to read a paper she and dad had had drawn up. I sat in the bedroom with them, and she handed me a will. It was in proper form and began with the usual sentences. Of course, they wanted all their debts paid and all expenses taken care of in the right manner— then all that was left of their worldly possessions was to come to me. Since I was an only child, this was very simple.

I sat holding the paper in my hands, and my mind went back over the years. My father died when I was about three. Several years later, my mother married again. She married one of the best men God ever let live. He was an official in The Methodist Church almost all his life, and the last few years before his illness, he was in charge of buildings and grounds for our home church. We never were well-to-do people, but there was always enough to eat and wear, though there were some hard days on the farm and in the little village after we left the farm. But there was never a request for help that went unanswered, whether deserved or not.

We lived by some definite rules, and they could be found in the Bible—the Ten Commandments, the Golden Rule, and the Beatitudes. I learned them early. Furthermore, church was never an option at our house, and when traveling evangelists came our way, we'd go hear them too. When I finished high school, college seemed like an impossibility. But the way opened, and there was always an extra dollar or two from home, saved for me instead of being spent on something I am sure my parents needed. There was never any grumbling about my being away in school while the family worked hard and dad put in overtime at the plant for extra pay.

As I sat and reminisced, this all seemed so long ago. After college came seminary, the first job, marriage to a lovely girl, and a family. All of this was made possible by the heritage that came from the right kind of home. There never was a lot of money or property, so they would not leave me much in "things," but my family had already given me more than I could ever repay: the heritage of happy memories and good habits and some lofty ideals and a religious faith. What more could any man want?

The most significant event in the world this moment is not what is happening in Viet Nam, or in the United Nations, or the Congress, or the Supreme Court—at any conference table, or in any laboratory. The most important event in any community is taking place in the delivery room of the hospital: the birth of a baby. For example, in the year 1809, Napoleon was running rampant across Europe, but Napoleon's wars were not the year's top stories. Charles Darwin was born that year. So was

Felix Mendelssohn, the great German composer. In any year, the most important event is the birth of a baby. Actually, the birth of every baby is another God-given chance to make the world a bit better. The greatest assets of any nation are the children and youth, for here is the hope that some of the mistakes of the older generation may be corrected by them.

The words expressed in our Scripture, Matthew 18:1,2, were written many years ago. Life was perilous for a child in the Roman Empire. The mortality rate was unbelievably high, and a Roman father had absolute power over his children—he could sell them as slaves, make them work as he pleased, punish them if he desired, and even kill them with impunity. A Roman son never came of age as long as his father lived. Even as a grown man, he remained under the power of his father. Frequently, unwanted children were just left to die, or were given away to kindly people, or sold for slaves. In 1 B.C., Hilarion wrote to his wife Alis from Alexandria: "If . . . you have a child, and it is a boy, let it live; if it is a girl, throw it out." Seneca wrote: ". . . children who are born weakly and deformed we drown."

It is true that the Hebrew people treated their children differently. They took pride in them and taught them the law and the prophets. But it came as a surprise to them when Jesus asked, "Who is the greatest in the kingdom of heaven?" and then called a little child and set him in the midst of them. The lesson was obvious. The qualities of the child were the qualities of heaven; the humility of the child was necessary to greatness; and to receive a little child was to receive the Lord himself. Then Jesus added a grave warning: "But whoso shall offend one of these little ones . . . better for him that a millstone were hanged about his neck, and that he were drowned in the depth of the sea" (Matthew 18:6). Throughout all of history the Christian Church has insisted on the importance of childhood. It has worked to do away with child labor, to make children safe on the streets, to get them out of the common jails with criminals, to provide the best in medicine and mental health care. When children have been left without parents, the church has stepped in with homes to provide what has been lost in love and care.

It is not easy to be a child today. We are moved to compassion when we see a hungry child anywhere in the world, but most of our children have enough of the necessities of life. Their chief lack arises from not being given a happy, wholesome, emotional environment in which to grow and develop. Some are denied any kind of understanding by parents. Often during counseling, young people say, "My parents wouldn't understand." Others receive no spiritual foundations, even from church-going parents. Some learn prejudices from prejudiced and bigoted parents. Other children have lost respect for themselves and their abilities because of domineering and ambitious parents, who want them to succeed for selfish reasons. Many a child has had dreams and hopes, only to lose them because there was no encouragement from parents, and others have been denied any form of discipline or guidelines for making decisions. I can readily understand what one child meant when she said, "I wish father would come home and make me behave." It seems to me that many homes are disorganized confusion. A woman had taught her Japanese helper, "Everything in its place, and a place for everything." Arriving home one day and finding the house in utter confusion, she asked the boy what she had taught him. He exploded, "Everything everyplace!" Homes are often like that morally and spiritually—just chaos.

Dr. David Smith thinks Paul wrote his immortal words, "Children, obey your parents . . . Honor thy father and mother . . . fathers do not provoke your children to anger . . ." (Eph. 6:1–4) out of bitter experience. "There is a quivering note of personal emotion," he wrote. Perhaps so. Many a man looks back on childhood, not as the happy time it ought to be, but with a sense of resentment and a feeling of having missed something very vital.

It is an inescapable fact that our children are what we are making them. When Woodrow Wilson was president of Princeton University, he said, "Some of you write and ask us why we don't make more of your boys. I will tell you the main reason: because they are your boys!" And Luther Burbank is reported to have said, "If we neglected our plants like we do our children, we would live in a wilderness of weeds."

We have spent a lot of time and energy castigating the Supreme Court of the United States on decisions about religion and the public schools. Nothing has been more misunderstood. In my judgment these decisions have placed the responsibility for the moral and spiritual training of children right where it belongs: in the family. I have had parents say to me, "We're not teachers. We'll keep Suzie well, safe, and healthy until she's old enough to go to kindergarten, and then we'll let trained teachers look after her training." But children aren't born in the kindergarten. They are born in the family, and the family is the first teacher in everything. Henry C. Link gives this classic illustration of a young man who said: "I have failed in business, I can't hold a job, and now I can't hold my wife. I have lost most of my friends and I can't even hang on to my money. I have had every advantage because my parents denied me nothing. They paid for my expensive college education, and they set me up in business. When I fell in love, they financed our marriage and our home. They did not want our marriage to suffer because of money worries. But now my marriage and everything else are ruined. I don't know where to turn. Everything has been done for me. I have about decided that there is something radically wrong with me." [1]

---

[1] Henry C. Link, *The Way To Security* (New York: Doubleday and Company, Inc., 1951), p. 23.

When Bishop Angie Smith was a little boy, a Negro woman looked after him. She called him "Bubber." One day she was in the yard with him, and he darted away from her. She called and called and finally found him. While she was hunting for him, Bishop Smith's mother heard the old Negro say, "They ain't hardly off your lap till they's on your heart!" We'd better get them on our hearts.

Here are five commandments for modern parents.

You shall remember that times change. This is a standing joke at our house. Sometimes, when Bill or Charles ask for something, or make some comment, I begin, "When I was a boy . . ." And they groan together, "Aw, Daddy!" Some things remain fixed, absolute, but these must be clothed in the language of the day and translated in terms of today's needs.

You shall remember that a good example is better than many words. So much of life is caught—taught by what we do rather than by what we say. In Brookhaven, Georgia, we lived across the street from a family with a pretty little girl. I enjoyed watching her parade down the sidewalk with her mother's shoes, hat, dress, and pocketbook—playing mother. Now that she is happily married and with children of her own, I am sure that she learned what it means to be a mother through the loving example of her own mother. Someone sent us a picture several years ago showing a father plodding through the snow. He turns to look, and with startled expression, sees his son following him—step by step. One of my favorite stories tells about a little boy who responded to a question about his age by saying, "I'm five at home, six at school, and three on the bus." Then, I once had another little seven-year-old friend who was the worst complainer I have ever known. He never felt well. A question about his health would trigger an organ recital. Where had he learned this attitude?—from his mother and dad. A good example is better than a book full of words.

You shall give your child encouragement. Martin Luther used to say, "Spare the rod and spoil the child— that is true; but beside the rod, keep an apple to give him when he has done well." Many children never hear the compliment when they have done a good job, but they get the scolding when they fail. Benjamin West describes how he became a painter. One day his mother left him with his sister, Sally. He found bottles of colored ink and painted Sally's portrait. In addition to the picture he managed to produce a real mess. When his mother came back, she saw it but said nothing. Picking up the paper he had been working on, she saw the painting and exclaimed, "Why it's Sally." And she rewarded his effort with a kiss. Benjamin West said, "My mother's kiss made me a painter." Children need to be encouraged to set high ideals and goals for themselves. Unfortunately, this is not a popular subject today. Idealism is frowned on in so many areas of contemporary life. But unless there are some dreams, ideals, goals, and unless our children and youth are encouraged to be and do their best, they will always be mediocre, or fail. When Abraham Lincoln's mother lay dying, her parting word to him was the simple encouragement, "Abe, be somebody!" This is our prayer for our boys, and then we encourage them in the pursuit of their goals.

You shall give your child freedom with love. Discipline is necessary. A child wants to know how far he can go, and he wants to know that someone cares if he goes wrong, or goes too far. Discipline is essential, but it is possible to exercise such control over children that their intelligence is insulted and their freedom to be persons is denied. Excessive restriction is an insinuation that we do not trust them. I had a close friend when I was a boy whose mother was like that. We would set out for the creek to swim and her parting word would be, "Now Clyde, don't you dare go near the water until you learn to swim!" Where was he to learn? On the coffee table?

Our love for our children must be unconditional, and our relationship is to be that of love-discipline. The one implies the other in the parent-child relationship. Whether they fail or achieve, are pretty or ugly, are mentally brilliant or average, we love them and we allow them freedom as they grow in the use of responsibility. A teen-age girl summed it up beautifully when her mother was about to give her a lecture on boy-girl relationships: "Mother, you can't slice life up that way. You can't take me off into a corner and say, 'Now daughter, we are going to talk about the boys!' I'll handle myself with boys in the same way you have taught me to handle myself everywhere else!" Teach your children to think and then let them think.

You shall introduce your child to God. Out of the mid-century White House Conference on Children and Youth came this statement: "We cannot insulate our children from the uncertainties of the world in which we move, or from the impact of the problems which confront us all. What we can do . . . is to equip them to meet these problems . . . to build up those inner resources of character which are the main strength of the American people." This is what J. Edgar Hoover had in mind when he said, "Parents must awaken to the realization that the family is the first great training school in behavior or misbehavior. Children develop a sense of right and wrong. They aren't born with it." It is not enough to provide children with food, clothes, a house, or even a good education. More important than any or all of these is an introduction to God as Father of all mankind, Creator, Sustainer, Giver of "every good and perfect gift." The very best thing we can do for our children is to introduce them to Jesus and help them make a commitment of their lives to him as Master and Lord. It is through him that we see God—

what he wants of us and how he loves us. And it is through him that life has meaning and purpose. The life of any child is empty, no matter how filled with things, until he has decided who will be his Master. None other is so able to be master as is Jesus Christ.

One day a Scottish minister was calling at the home of one of his church families. When the lady came to the door, he asked simply, "Does Jesus live here?" She did not answer, and he repeated the question, "Does Jesus live here?" The poor housewife was flustered and didn't know what to answer. The minister went his way. That evening she said to her husband, "John, the minister was here today, and he asked a curious question. He wanted to know if Jesus lived here."

John was irritated, and asked, "Didn't you tell him that we go to the church on the Lord's Day and put our money in the offering?"

"I was minded to say that, John, but he didn't ask that. He asked, 'Does Jesus live here?' and John, that is different!" How important that Jesus live in our homes, so that he becomes the regular companion of our children. Children love heroes, in fact are hero-worshipers. How simple to set Jesus up as the hero of every boy and girl and bring them to the point of commitment to a person, the best person ever to live—the Son of God—our Savior—our living Lord.

> Happy the home where Jesus' name
> Is sweet to every ear;
> Where children early lisp his fame,
> And parents hold him dear.[2]

It was graduation down in the Ozarks. The honor graduate was a boy named Eddie. He was the son of a

---

[2] Henry Ware, Jr., "Happy The Home When God Is There," *The Methodist Hymnal* (Nashville: The Methodist Publishing House, 1964, 1966), p. 516.

farmer father and mother who had never been far away from home. It was quite an event for them to travel by train to the college campus for the commencement. But go they must, for their Eddie was to give the major address. They came and sat on the very back seat, for they were self-conscious and embarrassed. Father's suit was shiny, and mother's dress was very plain. They sat in awed silence through the proceedings. Eddie got up to speak, and he spoke with ease and eloquence, for he was a brilliant boy. The father and mother felt they were seeing a different son from the one they had known on the farm. Tears blinded them as their boy told what his home and country and school and church had meant to him, and how he and his classmates were now going out to save the things they loved. When the speech ended, the old man, sentimental for the first time in years, grasped his wife's hand and stammered, "Maw, that boy is the best crop we ever grew." How true! Our best crop as parents is to "grow" good sons and daughters and send them out to make a better world.

6

The Trouble With This

Younger Generation . . .

Children, obey your parents in the Lord, for this is right. Honor thy father and mother . . . Ephesians 6:1–2
. . . but bring them up in the discipline and instruction of the Lord. Ephesians 6:4, RSV

There *is* something new under the sun—it is called "the generation gap." Actually, we've always had it, but it has never been as pronounced as now. It may be defined as that gap in the understanding between young people and adults. In *West Side Story*, a young person says to an adult, "You were never our age!" All young people have either said it, or shown it in attitudes toward adults.

A teen-ager wrote an essay in which he said, "The world is full of people who keep saying, 'I was a boy once,' but who never show any signs of it!"

Times do change. Recently, we were vacationing at Lake Hartwell for a few days. When I put on walking shorts, our Bill, age 13 (going on 20), looked at me critically, and said, "Dad, the world isn't ready for that!"

Recently, I read about a policeman who saw a man sitting on the steps of a house at three o'clock in the morning. He wanted to know what the man was doing. "I've lost my key, and I'm waiting for my children to come home and let me in!"

Times change. I have been teaching a class on values in the youth division of our church. On the first Sunday, I commented on the fact that when I was a boy we were not allowed to do a certain thing. A pretty little girl put me in my place by saying, "But you were then. We are now."

The problem of the yawning gulf between young people and adults is more serious today than at any time before. More is said and less understood about teen-agers than ever before in history. The problem seems to reach its peak at about sixteen or seventeen, and then increases! A mother said in a family class recently, "My favorite verse in the Bible is, 'It came to pass!'" Understandable. At six, children know all the questions. At sixteen, the teen-ager knows all the answers! Someone has defined an adolescent as "an *it* turning into a *he* or a *she*." A boy becomes an adult three years before his parents think so, and two years after he thinks he does. Having a teen-ager at our house, I know what the man meant when he said, "The older generation thought nothing of getting up at six in the morning. The younger generation doesn't think much of it either."

But you know, the main trouble I find with the younger generation is that I don't belong to it any more. I am convinced that our problems with young people are not due nearly as much to downright badness as to downright confusion. Most of the youth I know want to do right, once they discover what is right. A cartoon in a recent magazine showed a group of young people dancing. When the music stopped, the girl said to the boy who stood before her, "Thanks for dancing with me." The boy replied, "I wasn't dancing. I was trying to get past you to the coke machine." Frequently, the problem is confusion, not badness.

Bishop Hazen G. Werner suggests, that we stop trying to prescribe cures for young people and start trying to understand them. This is what Richard McCann meant when he said, "It is not sufficient to know the delinquent's deed; we must know the delinquent." [1]

The teen-ager shrinks from life's demands and yet desires to push forward. He feels insecure, but he has a sense of certainty about himself, and he finds himself more and more out of the comfortable, protective lines. There is a disdain for authority. Betty McDonald has commented, "They are going to be miserable no matter what they are doing, but they would rather be miserable doing the things they choose."

Independence is developing faster than the capacity to handle it. The young person is moving from self-centeredness to social and vocational responsibility. Above all things, he wants approval, meaning, and love from parents and peers. The tragedy is, far too many young people never experience love or approval, especially on the part of parents. Dr. Wanda Walker wrote: "A study of maladjusted teen-agers recently conducted in a large city high school in Oklahoma by a team of counselors shows how it is important to tell our children that we love them. After the counselors had worked long enough to gain rapport and confidence of ten of the students who were the most maladjusted in the school, they asked them how long it had been since their parents had told them that they loved them. Not a single one could ever remember having heard such a comment. By contrast, the counselor visited with ten of those considered best adjusted and well

---

[1] Richard McCann, *Delinquency: Sickness or Sin* (New York: Harper and Brothers Company, 1957).

accepted, the outstanding leaders in the high school, and asked the same question. Without exception, they answered either 'this morning' or 'last night' or indicated that they had been verbally reassured of their parents' love within the past few hours."[2]

I believe that if young people are assured they are loved, no matter what they do, are accepted, no matter what they do, and are disciplined when necessary, they will grow to emotional maturity and social usefulness. Many of the young people I see who have run away from home—hippies, as well as others—have done so because they do not feel loved, understood, or even wanted. Many have been bored with traditional family living patterns and have turned to alcohol, drugs, smoking, and a variety of other things for excitement.

Dr. D. C. Williams said, "You don't need to be right all the time. Your child wants a man for a father, not a formula. He wants a woman for a mother, not a theory. He wants real parents, real people, capable of making mistakes without moping about it."

Dr. Viktor E. Frankl writes: "In my opinion man is dominated neither by the will to pleasure (Freud), nor by the will to power (Adler) but by what I call the will-to-meaning; that is to say, his deepest striving and struggle for a higher and ultimate meaning to his existence. This is his mission in life, his unique task."[3] This is where the struggle goes on with the teen-ager: a struggle to find meaning, love, purpose in life.

This search is expressed in their music. Simon and Garfunkel have discovered the mood in such hits as

---

[2] Wanda Walker, "Children Absorb Mental and Emotional Health," *The Christian Home,* February 1964, p. 10.

[3] Viktor E. Frankl, *Man's Search for Meaning* (New York: Washington Square Press, 1963).

"Sounds of Silence," "I Am A Rock," and "Mrs. Robinson." And in such music as "Too Much Talk And Not Enough Action," by Paul Revere and the Raiders.

There are many reasons for the generation gap. For one thing, the world of today is so completely different from the world that I knew as a young person. I can remember the flight of Charles A. Lindbergh . . . our daily paper came out by rural carrier, and I could hardly wait to read what had happened. It was usually several days after the event before we knew the details. During the Second World War, radio brought us up-to-date reports. Now, we can actually watch the launching of a space craft that travels around the globe in ninety minutes. We can view the accounts of the day's fighting in foreign conflicts as they happen. There is so much about the physical world today that is different from the world we knew as young people.

The same pace of change has taken place in the realm of morals and ethics. There seem to be no clearly defined standards of conduct. Parents are as mixed up as their children. Even religion can be a confusing factor, interpreted as it is in so many different ways. Morals are not pictured in white or black. There appears to be a tendency to do away with rules and discipline. "It's my life and I'll do as I please" is commonly heard. "Don't fence me in" is more than a song title of two decades ago; it has become a philosophy of life practiced by a multitude of people. *Time* magazine has described our era as one "in which pleasure is increasingly considered an almost constitutional right rather than a privilege, in which self-denial is increasingly seen as foolishness rather than virtue." This is why youth are confused. So are adults. The moral and ethical world of today differs from that of a generation ago.

Another contributing factor is our utter dependence on

things. Things are in the saddle and ride mankind! Young people are richer than ever before. They own more cars, have more money to spend, have greater educational opportunities, and possess more vocational opportunities than any previous generation. Young people spend more than ten billion dollars a year on a multitude of things. It is no wonder that television, magazine, and radio advertising is slanted to them. There are more than sixty-five million people in our country under eighteen, and by 1975, it is estimated that half our population will be under twenty-five. It is easy to understand why manufacturers concentrate on this market. More is said about youth, more planned for them, more done for them than ever before. This tends to create problems—a sense of confusion and a false sense of superiority.

Still another factor is this: we live in a world where 90% of our knowledge in physical and biological sciences has come in less than thirty years. A doctor told me recently that our knowledge of medicine would double in five years. And the same may be said of almost every other field. There is so much to know and so many opportunities for discovery and exploration that youth are confused by the enormity of it all, especially since they are thrust into it so suddenly and so completely. The bulldozer has become the symbol of our age. Everything is in a state of change. Nothing seems to stay put. How hard to imagine how difficult it is for a boy to decide on a career. How can he best use his abilities? Should he concentrate on making money or serving mankind—or can both be accomplished at once? Where should he go to school? What should his guiding principles in life be? These are hard decisions in a changing world.

The generation gap is a fact, though it is not really new. Several years ago the *New York Post* carried some comments under the by-line of Eleanor Roosevelt: "It might be encouraging to many of us who worry about the state

of our world and particularly about our youngsters to remember that today's problems have existed a long time." [4]
She then referred to the following quotations: "Our earth
is degenerate in these latter days; bribery and corruption
are common; children no longer obey their parents; the
end of the world is evidently approaching" (quotation
from an Assyrian Stone Tablet, c. 2800 B.C.).

"Children now love luxury; they have bad manners,
contempt for authority. Children are now tyrants, not the
servants of their households. They contradict their parents, chatter before company, gobble up dainties at the
table, tyrannize their teachers" (Plato quoting Socrates).

The generation gap is not new, but it is dangerous and
challenging.

Religion has a word for us here. Paul, in his Ephesian
letter, places the responsibility equally on parent and
child. "Children, obey your parents in the Lord, for this is
right. Honor your father and mother" (Ephesians 6:1–2).
"But bring them up in the discipline and instruction of the
Lord" (Ephesians 6:4, RSV). This is so. There is no substitute for the Christian faith as it is developed in the
family relationship. I see mottoes hanging on walls in
some homes that read, "Christ is the head of this house!"
If it were so in more and more homes, from the very
establishment of the home, much of the trouble with the
generation gap could be eliminated. There is no substitute
for a common love for Christ to give us a foundation
on which to stand and from which to move to solve the
problem of the generations.

For one thing, Christ helps us understand that each
person is different, each has worth and dignity in his
own right, and that age does not matter. God never made

---

[4] Eleanor Roosevelt, "What Is The World Coming To?" *The
New York Post.* Copyright 1961 by United Feature Syndicate,
Inc.

two things alike: neither leaves nor persons. Each is separate and distinct, with its own characteristics. It has been said that God loves us each as if he did not have another in all the world to love. How easy it is for one of us to think he has a corner on knowledge or rights, but wisdom did not come to the world with any one of us, and it will not go when we do. A freshman class paraded down the street of the university town carrying banners saying, "This university has waited two hundred years for us." How absurd! Each age—youth, maturity, old age —has its own beauty and worth, and Christ helps us see that fact and appreciate each for what he is.

In the second place, Christ helps us see that we need each other for fullfillment. In "A Solitary Way," whose author is unknown, there are these lines.

> There is a mystery in human hearts,
> And though we be encircled by a host
> Of those who love us well and are beloved,
> To every one of us from time to time,
> There comes a sense of utter loneliness.

No man is an island actually. The Bible says in unmistakable terms: "No man lives to himself and no man dies to himself." And Jesus said, "Love!" Love implies an object upon which to lavish itself. I remember hearing Bishop Hazen G. Werner tell of a letter a mother showed him from her son in Korea. He was soon to come home, and he told his mother all the endearing things a boy wants to say. He told her of his homecoming and said that on the first night he wanted the kind of supper that only she could fix. And mothers have a way of knowing how to pamper the tastes of a boy—if he'll only let her. Then he said that after supper he wanted the family to sit around and "thank God for the privilege of being together again!"

How desperately we need each other. A prodigal son in a far country remembered the father's house with nos-

talgia. We seem to think it important to assert ourselves—
to be independent, but it is different when the chips are
down. I have talked with many young people who have
run away from the restrictions of home—from New York,
or San Francisco, or Tracy City—because mom and dad
didn't understand. Again and again they have wanted to
know how to go about working things out to go home!
They have come to realize how wrong they were and have
accepted the fact that much of the fault was theirs.

Yes, we need each other, and we ought to admit it
every day. Christ helps us see that we cannot possibly
stand alone. When he comes to live in our lives, we see
each other in new light. Mistrust and ill will are so blind
that they can never see what can be for being mad at
what is. Jesus saw in Matthew, the tax collector, a faithful
disciple. He saw in a drunk on the street curb, a Billy
Sunday. He saw in a humble Negro slave, a George Washington Carver. Christ enables us to see each other through
different eyes and to perceive our need for each other.

Finally, Christ empowers us to bridge the generation
gap. John fairly shouted, "To as many as received him,
to them gave he power to become the sons of God."
Power! We have so emphasized the power of machines
that we have lost sight of the power of God in our lives—
that spiritual power that enables us to use all other pow-
ers in the right way. Grace Noll Crowell put it beautifully:

> So long as there are homes where fires burn
> And there is bread;
> So long as there are homes where lamps are lit
> And prayers are said;
> Although people falter through the dark—
> And nations grope—
> With God himself back of these little homes—
> We have sure hope.[5]

[5] Grace Noll Crowell, *Light of The Years* (New York: Harper and Brothers, 1936).

I believe that faith in Christ is a cure-all for the problems of the family. Age has nothing to do with it. Christ can be real and powerful in the life of a child, a teen-ager, or an adult. Through his power we can bridge all gaps, heal all wounds. Edward White, one of the three astronauts killed in the explosion at Cape Kennedy, said of his parents: "When I was a boy, I don't suppose I had a more lively interest in faith than most youngsters. But I had parents who knew how to communicate their own beliefs in terms I could understand. My brother Jim and my sister Jean and I never doubted where our parents stood on the question of religion. The Bible in our home was not a book to sit on the shelf; it was out where it could be used. Church was not a seasonal affair; going to church on Sunday was as much a part of the rhythm of life as washing the clothes on Monday." [6] And vital faith, practiced day in and out gives us a foundation on which to stand, and one from which to move to bridge any gaps that separate us.

[6] From *Methodist Messenger*, First United Methodist Church, Ann Arbor, Michigan, May 23, 1968.

7

◥◥◥◥◥◥◥◥

Where Does Daddy Come In?

Dr. Edward A. Strecker, a psychiatrist, tells of a father, a very wealthy man in a high government post, who came to his office one day.

"I have two sons," he said briskly, "and they are fine boys but a little wild. Always getting expelled from school and that sort of thing. They need a father's guidance. Their mother is a good woman and loves them very much, but she spoils them. I'm afraid they won't grow up to be real men.

"Unfortunately, I can't spend much time with them for I have had to put my duty to the nation before everything else. My idea is that you, in effect, should be their father. Take full charge. I'll pay you anything you ask. It would be worth a great deal to me to know that my boys were in your care."

"Regretfully, I had to say no. 'It's not that I don't want the job.' I told him. 'Your boys need a father all right, but no substitute will do. It seems to me your first responsibility to this country is to develop your sons into upstanding, well-balanced, responsible young citizens. Nothing you accomplish in Washington can possibly be more important!'

"After I turned down his suggestion, he insisted on sending his sons to a strict boys' school in order, as he put it, 'that they may be exposed to strong male influences.' The school was a good one, but teachers, however conscientious, cannot substitute for a father. The boys were even then struggling with emotional problems caused mainly by their lopsided family life.

"At school they developed further difficulties that would have been instantly apparent to the watchful eye of a father but went unnoticed by the indulgent mother and the busy teachers. The boys are now 17 and 19. The younger is a drug addict, struggling with a serious problem of adjustment that verges on homosexuality. The other is a thief. Even his influential father will not be able to keep him out of prison much longer." [1]

Children need a father. Recently we attended the funeral of a very fine young father who left behind four sons. Several times, while we were visiting with friends before the funeral, they said, "These boys sure will miss him. Every boy needs a daddy!" And so do girls, too! All children need a father in the best sense of that word. For too many fathers it runs like this: "Sure, I cooperated in producing this child. But when I got through pacing the hospital floor, my part was finished. In the last ten years I've paid the bills. Sure, I'm fond of the kid. Proud of him too. Suppose I should take more time with him. But my wife can take him to the zoo as well as I can, and she knows more of the answers than I do anyway." Unfortunately, that may be true, but the answers a woman gives are of necessity one-sided. The society your child is destined to grow up in is both male and female. Your son needs a man around that he can respect and

---

[1] Edward A. Strecker, "The Vanishing American Father," *This Week* magazine, 1949.

imitate. Daughters need a father too. He sets the pattern for the daughter's future judgment in men. If she picks out a husband you consider not good enough, remember that she got her ideal of manhood from you! If a father is a godly and happy man, the daughter is likely to pick out that kind of man for a husband. Better than any lectures about being home at a reasonable hour, being selective about the choice of friends, and being clean and pure of body is the example of a father who is all of these things.

A little girl said to her mother one day: "Mama, if I don't marry will I be an old maid like Aunt Mary?"

"Yes, dear," replied mother.

Then the child said, "Mama, if I marry will I get a husband like daddy?"

"Yes, dear."

After some thought, the little girl said, "Mama, it sure is a tough world on us women!"

I heard recently about a mother who thought her husband was not much of a man. She made every effort to divert her son's admiration from the father to a swashbuckling uncle who made his living leveling mountains and building roads and bridges. A guest in the home said to the boy, "I guess you are going to be a great engineer like your uncle." "No," replied the boy, "I guess I'll be a neurotic like my father!" Children get their ideas and ideals of life from what they see and hear at home, particularly from the father. And sadly enough, many fathers are in full retreat from parental duties!

It is true that there are unavoidable pressures of living these days that make it difficult for father to have much time with the children. A boy said to his mother, "Mother, when I die will I go to heaven?" "That's what the Bible teaches, son," replied the mother. "When you die will you go to heaven?" "Yes, son." The boy was silent for a time, then said, "It's too bad Daddy can't go, isn't it?" "What in the world do you mean?" his mother asked. "He'll be too busy working to go," said the boy.

Some men are sergeant types: Home is their castle and they must be obeyed regardless of anything. Others are indulgent, giving in when they ought to give out, leaving discipline to mother. Some fathers think that to earn money and bring home the bacon is all that is necessary. Yes, there are all kinds of fathers, but I want to discuss the ideal father.

The ideal father is patient with his children and spends time with them. No part of child guidance is of more importance than assuring your child, by action and word, that he is important to the family and has a place in your affections. "Would you like to know what I am giving my son for Christmas?" asked a prominent businessman. He showed me a piece of paper on which was written: "To my son: I give you one hour of each weekday and two hours of my Sundays, to be used as you wish!"

This is the greatest gift a father can give.

It means learning to listen to the children, to work patiently with them, to teach them the real meaning of life. If you want your son to learn a handcraft skill, you do not hand him a tool kit and say go down in the basement and build a boat. You go with him, draw plans, buy materials, look at pictures, and build.

When you paint the porch, do you give your son a quarter and tell him to run along to the movies or do you give him a paintbrush and risk having paint all over the house? When you plant flowers, do you invite little Suzie to help even though she eats up the seed? After all, the best way to teach children good work habits and how to cooperate with others is in the home.

And there are the questions! Someone has estimated that a child will ask 500,000 questions before he is fifteen years old. A little boy was asking his father questions. "What makes the grass green? . . . What makes the sky blue? . . . Where does the wind come from? . . . What holds the clouds up?" To each question the father responded, "I don't know!" Finally, the boy said, "Daddy, am I bothering you with my questions?" "No, son, how do you expect to learn anything if you don't ask questions?" replied father. The ideal father is patient with his children, listening to their questions and responding creatively.

A boy, twenty-one years old, stood before the judge for sentencing. The judge shamed him for his behavior and reminded him of his father who had been a famous judge. The boy spoke, "My father never had time for me, and when I came to him for help, he was always busy. He never helped me, never gave me advice. He is responsible for me being here!"

Gipsy Smith, the gifted evangelist of an earlier generation, was busy in his study one day when one of his sons entered the room. He offered him a number of things: knife, quarter, pencil—all to no avail. Finally he asked, "Son, what do you want?" The boy replied, "Daddy, I just want you!"

The ideal father is firm. He knows the child must learn obedience. Unless he learns obedience as a child, he will be a miserable misfit, since life is made up of rules and laws. A judge in Chicago said that parents are to blame for the large number of children in the juvenile courts. "Parents permit their children to do things which they themselves do not approve, but they have the passive attitude, and no backbone. Just a lack of parental oversight makes them the sort of boys and girls they are." Parents need to be firm and understanding, but not cruel. Children want to know the rules. They appreciate discipline, if it is firm and honest—and given in love.

In addition to patience and firmness, the ideal father has a sympathy for his children. This is love. It means he is interested in everything that interests them—a report card, a boy friend, a party, what happened at the swimming pool or in Sunday school. It seems to me this was one of President Kennedy's greatest attributes. He found time every day for his children, romping with them, boating with them, telling them stories. Busy as he was, he tried to enter sympathetically into their lives.

Contrast that with the farmer who instructed his son late one afternoon to milk the cows, feed the horses, slop the pigs, gather the eggs, catch the colt, split some kindling, stir the cream, pump fresh water, study your lessons, and then go to bed. In the meantime the father went off to a meeting to discuss the question: "How shall we keep our sons on the farm?" What an example!

Our children need our sympathetic interest and concern. They have problems. Remember, they are not simply sawed-off adults, but their problems are peculiar to them, and just as real as any adult problems can be. Often the one thing they need is to feel that someone understands and cares for them. An attitude of sympathy is the best answer to many a problem. Rufus Jones wrote about his boyhood in the book, *A Small Town Boy:* "But there was something more to our family religion than this morning devotion together. The life in our home was saturated with the reality and the practice of love. We spoke to each other as though love were ruling and guiding us. I cannot remember that mother ever shouted or scolded. She was often grieved, I know. Her face had a look of sadness, but she was tender in her sadness, and she conquered my stubborn nature and my thoughtlessness which was worse, not by scolding words, and not by whipping me, but by looking at me in her way. I could stand anything but that. It was an old-fashioned home where nurture went on all the time. It was a life building center. It was here that my anchors were forged." [2] Love and sympathy. How essential these qualities are in the early years if a child is to have stability throughout all of life. To know that one is loved and appreciated, respected for what he is, is one of life's greatest blessings whether we be ten or sixty.

And the final thing is this: the ideal father is Christian. He sets an example of godliness before his children. A father's interest in his children must transcend the requirements for providing physical needs alone. Children have minds to be trained, spirits to be nurtured in the fear and admonition of the Lord, talents to be recognized and developed. A father can, by his own spirit and life, help his children to come into such knowledge, understanding, and spirit that will let them "see life steady and see it whole." Lord Chesterfield wrote his son: "Dear Boy: From the time that you have had life, it has been the principle and favorite object of mine to make you as perfect as the imperfections of human nature will allow; in this view I have grudged no pains, nor expense in your education . . . While you were a child, I endeavored to form your heart habitually to virtue and honor before your understanding was capable of showing you their beauty and utility . . ."

The greatest bequest any father can give his child is that of a love for God, a faith in Jesus Christ, a knowledge of the Bible, an understanding of prayer, and a desire to be a part of and work in the church. Every father has the privilege of leading his children to be Christians, not just in name but in actuality.

A young man in his late teens was desperately ill. His father sat by his bedside as life ebbed away. The boy had

---

[2] Rufus M. Jones, *A Small Town Boy* (New York: The Macmillan Company, 1941), pp. 32, 33.

had everything money could buy: cars, trips, pets, education. The boy turned to his father and said, "You've been a good father to me. You've given me everything a father could give his son. But now I'm dying, and I'm afraid. You never told me about God!"

Home is the beginning place of Christian faith. Don't expect the Christian Education Department of any church to do in forty-five minutes a week what you ought to be doing all the time. An ideal father is a Christian, and seeks to lead every member of his family into a vital relationship with Christ.

8

¥¥¥¥¥¥¥¥

A Christian Attitude Toward Sex

Genesis 2:18–25; I Corinthians 5:15–20

An old retired Methodist preacher was asked to perform the wedding of his granddaughter. For years before he retired he had never held a book in his hand during a wedding ceremony, and he insisted that he could do the ritual now without any help. The granddaughter wanted him to have his manual with him in case he needed it. But he persisted, and things went well for the first few sentences: "Dearly beloved, we are gathered in the sight of God and in the presence of witnesses to join together John and Mary in holy matrimony. Which is an honorable estate, instituted of God, and signifying unto us that mystical union which exists between Christ and His Church." Then his mind went blank. He backed up and started over again, but he forgot his lines at the same place. Finally, after a third attempt, he leaned over the chancel rail and said, "What it means kids, is that it ain't to be tampered with." And so it is with the subject before us.

No subject is more discussed or less understood than sex. It is involved in everything in our modern living: advertising, movies, novels, normal conversation. We think we have all the answers. Sex is supposed to be a sophisticated matter in our times. In the new morality there are no absolutes except love. Gael Greene points out in the book, *Sex and the College Girl,* that the direction everywhere is toward a loose attitude toward this relationship,[1] and a college chaplain said last year in a sermon on his campus, "Sex is fun. There are no rules!"

We in the church have failed to face honestly up to this matter out of fear of embarrassing some timid soul, or of saying something contrary to popularly held ideas, or simply because we did not have the knowledge. By our timidity we have given the impression that sex is sinful and the body is evil. As parents, we have objected to the teaching of this subject in the public schools. Recently, we offered a sensible course on the subject in our church on Sunday evenings for some of our young people. Two mothers came to me and said, "We wish you'd stick to religion in the church." But parents don't tell their children the facts at home. A father said to his son at dinner. "After dinner, I want to talk to you about the facts of life. Wait for me in the living room." After dinner, the father went into the living room and was greeted with the question, "O.K. Pop, what do you want to know?"

The time comes when the church must, because of the situation, say what its position is. With a continual increase in divorce, venereal disease, children born out of wedlock, and abortions, the church ought to have something to say about a part of life that is so vital.

Some time ago, an Italian film depicted the city of Rome as one of the most corrupt in the world. The film, *La Dolce Vita* directed by Federico Fellini, showed what happens to people and to society when the attitude

---

[1]Gael Greene, *Sex and the College Girl* (New York: Dial Press, Inc., 1964).

toward sex is loose. Fellini chose characters from the elite set in Rome and traced them through twenty-four hours of obscenity and debauchery. In one of the last scenes, a dozen people sit in a room and stare at each other, completely bored. Everything has been tried, and they sit in silent disgust. The last scene is a parable. These same people are standing on the seashore looking at a fish that has washed ashore during the night. It is perfectly round. There is no distinction between head and tail. Thus Fellini describes the vicious circle of illicit sex: frustration, boredom, despair. Standing to one side is a girl dressed in white, representing purity. She keeps calling, "Come back! Come back!" Our age plays it fast and loose with sex, but deep in our subconscious there is a voice that keeps calling to us, "Come back, Come back!"

Let me tell you first of all what the Christian attitude toward sex is not.

There are at least five popularly held ideas that the Christian cannot accept.

1. Sex is just physical, a natural appetite which needs satisfying like the need for food, and has nothing to do with the rest of life. A popular philosophy may say that there is no moral or ethical connotation to the sex act. It is like taking a drink of water.

2. Love covers all things. If two people love each other, let them go ahead just as if married—love makes this relationship beautiful.

3. Young people must learn, and the best way to learn is by experience. Premarital relationships help in adjustment in future marriage. This myth is exploded by doctors. Almost any two people in the world can adjust sexually, all else being equal! Experimentation is simply an excuse for license.

4. To suppress the natural desire is psychologically dangerous.

5. Moral laws are relative to the times and the situation. There are no absolutes except love. Morality is dictated by society and not by God.

By the same token, the Christian position is not one of prudery. It is not the old Victorian idea that the body is evil.

What then is the Christian position?

1. God is the creator of all things. He made us as we are. "In the beginning God created the heaven and the earth . . . And God said, Let us make man in our image, after our likeness: and let them have dominion over the fish of the sea, and over the fowl of the air, and over the cattle, and over all the earth, and over every creeping thing that creepeth upon the earth. So God created man in his own image, in the image of God created he him; male and female created he them. And God blessed them, and God said unto them, Be fruitful, and multiply, and replenish the earth, and subdue it: and have dominion over the fish of the sea, and over the fowl of the air, and over every living thing that moveth upon the earth . . . Therefore shall a man leave his father and mother, and shall cleave unto his wife: and they shall be one flesh" (Genesis 1:1, 26, 27, 28; 2:24). You cannot separate man into body and soul. He is all tied up in one bundle of life. The Christian Church maintains that sex is good, not evil —man perverts sex. It is instituted of God for the continuation of the human race, and it is given by God to meet certain psychological needs that cannot be met otherwise. It is the highest consummation of love between two people. In a sense, it is a sacrament. Sex becomes the supreme language of love. Physical union is the expression of an inward and spiritual grace.

Alan Paton, in his novel *Too Late The Phalarope*, expresses an old idea in modern language. Pieter is speaking.

His wife, a strict Protestant, is unable to love him completely in a physical way because she thinks the body is evil and that she should be spiritual. He says to her: "It's all together, the body, and soul, and mind, between a man and a woman. When you love me as you've done, I'm comforted in them all. And when I love you as I've done, it's you I love, your body and mind and soul." Later on he says, "And I wanted to cry out at her that I could not put the body apart from the soul, and that the comfort of her body was more than a thing of the flesh, but was also a comfort of the soul, and why it was, I could not say, and why it should be, I could not say, but there was nothing in it that was ugly or evil, only good!" [2] That's what the Bible says, put in modern language.

The church teaches chastity before marriage and faithfulness afterwards, not to be narrow or puritanical, but because the sex relationship is not just physical, but spiritual, involving all of a person. You cannot fully love more than one person, and to give yourself to a variety of persons cheapens the creation of God. God created us as persons of worth and dignity—mind, soul, body—and for his glory. How we treat our own bodies and that of other persons is an indication of how we treat God. For the Christian, the sex act is the symbol of love, "till death do us part!"

2. Sex involves persons. We have dehumanized sex and made it an object. We see people as things not as persons. And when we do, we can use the bodies of others to satisfy our own lusts without any concern for what it does to them or to society. This is the great danger of the Playboy philosophy, epitomized in Hugh Hefner. He mailed out letters to people all over the country setting forth this idea—women are sex symbols and are to be

---

[2] Alan Paton, *Too Late the Phalarope* (New York: Scribner's, 1953).

exploited for physical enjoyment. Nothing will destroy a nation as quickly as the Playboy philosophy where persons are seen only as things, as objects. Self-love and self-gratification are the chief characteristics of this philosophy. "I love me and want you!" The Bible teaches the sacredness of the total person: "Know ye not that your body is the temple of the Holy Ghost . . . ?" (1 Corinthians 6:19).

3. Sex requires social responsibility. Marriage is always implicated in sex. Sex is the link to the past and with the future. No Christian can enter into this relationship without a deep sense of the mystery of the continuation of life. The real sickness in the sexual revolution is "love," apart from marriage responsibility. *Look* magazine carried a report of a survey made among one hundred young adults. It was not a representative survey, but the results were startling. One student was asked about his various night activities. Was love the real object? Here is his reply: "Love? You must be kidding. Sex. Good old healthy sex is what I want. I don't need love." [3] He distinguished between love and sex: "Sex is conquest. Love is surrender. Who wants surrender?" And this philosophy threatens to destroy our country: *no sense of responsibility!* Love is responsibility. Love is loyalty. Love is sacrifice. Love is devotion. For the sex relationship to have real and vital meaning, it requires the continuity and responsibility and fullfillment of marriage. This is the meaning of the Bible: "For this cause . . ." (Mark 10: 7–9). Sex is not something done in a dark corner. It is never private. It is always public in effect and responsibility. From it comes the family, and in the family are reproduced attitudes and ideas that affect all the human race.

---

[3] *Look* magazine, Vol. 1, No. 2. Quoted from sermon by Dr. L. Bevel Jones, First Methodist Church, Decatur, Georgia.

To control this powerful force in us, a personal relationship with God is essential

The General Assembly of the Presbyterian Church, U.S., meeting in Winston Salem in 1962 reported: "Like a river without banks, the wrong expression of this natural desire can get out of bounds, creating a swamp which becomes a breeding place for disease and misery. Kept within the confining banks of God's laws and love, it can be a mighty force for man's individual happiness as well as for the well-being of society and the strengthening of family ties."

Dr. J. Wallace Hamilton wrote a book entitled *Ride the Wild Horses*. He compares the basic human instincts to a wild horse that must be tamed. In sex, some people advocate letting the wild horses run. Others say, eliminate sex, break the wild horses, or eliminate the horse. The Christian way is neither self-negation, nor self-assertion. It is self-fulfillment. A wild horse can be trained until rider and horse work perfectly together. So spirit and body can be brought under control and used together for self-fulfillment.[4]

No person can handle the temptations of sex alone, but with God's help there is no temptation you cannot handle. Turn again to the story of Joseph in Genesis 29. The Bible describes the bedroom scene. Joseph won the favor of Potiphar and was given great responsibility. Potiphar left him in charge of everything. He had the run of the house. When Potiphar was gone, his wife would try every way she knew to induce Joseph to go to bed with her. But do you remember his answer? He didn't say, "I might catch some disease!" Nor did he say, "We might have a baby!" His refusal was rooted in his faith: "How then

---

[4] J. Wallace Hamilton, *Ride the Wild Horses* (Westwood, N.J.: Fleming H. Revell, 1952).

can I do this great wickedness, and sin against God?" This is the secret of our success in temptation, this one or any other: a strong faith in God that sees him as creator of all that is, that sees every human being as having dignity and worth, and that has a sense of social responsibility.

But suppose we have failed at this point and have given in to temptation by being unchaste or unfaithful. Is there hope? Remember the girl in white calling "Come back! Come back!" We can come back to God no matter what our sin. No sex sin is unpardonable. To the woman taken in adultery, Jesus said, "Neither do I condemn you. Go and sin no more." I wish I knew all that happened after that, but of one thing I am certain—she didn't do it again. By the love of God we are transformed, no matter what our sin. John reminds us forcefully, "If we confess our sins he is faithful and just to forgive us our sins and to cleanse us from all unrighteousness" (I John 1:9). That applies to every sin in the book. Any person can climb from the road of lust to the high road of love by a vital faith in Jesus Christ.

Harry H. Kreuner tells a story about O. Henry, in his book, *Specifically To Youth*. O. Henry's real name was Sydney Porter. He was put in jail for embezzlement when he was a young man. While in prison, Porter met a guard named Oren Henry. When the time came for him to leave prison, rather than take his old name which was badly besmirched by his crime, he took the name of the guard and called himself O. Henry. His marvelous stories were written under that name. As he left the prison, the old guard waved to him and said, "Take good care of our name!" [5]

What is our name? Our name is Man. We are made in the likeness of God. He is our Father. "Take good care of our name," he says.

---

[5] Harry H. Kruener, *Specifically to Youth* (New York: Harper and Brothers, 1959).

9

Frayed And Frustrated Or
Finished And Fruitful!

They shall still bring forth fruit in old age; they shall be fat and flourishing. Psalms 92:14

There is one way to avoid old age: die young! It is perfectly normal to get older, but we treat it as a disease. There are some who feel that if any age in life is a disease, it is youth—old age is getting over it.

Many people try to fight old age, camouflage it, or deny it. Certainly, the later years do have their minus side. I was preaching in South Georgia several years ago and made the statement that life after forty is characterized by four B's: bulges, bifocals, baldness, and bridges. An older woman sitting in the congregation piped up and said, "Preacher, don't forget my bunions!" But each stage in life has its own beauty and rewards, and the later years of life have theirs. A woman said to me recently, "I have been completely happy since I stopped trying to look and act twenty years younger and began acting my age!" Dr. B. M. Kirkland said once, "Wrinkles are only the by-paths of many smiles, and some tears; gray hair is the silver dust of the stars; and growing gracefully slower of step is only walking nearer and closer to God." Someone asked John Barrymore on his seventieth birthday if acting was as much fun at seventy as at forty. He replied, "My friend, nothing is as much fun at seventy as at forty!" The years after sixty-five may not be as glamorous as the years before, and yet, these later years in life can be fun, interesting, and fruitful in many ways.

The advances of science have lengthened our lives. In 1900, the life expectancy for a woman was fifty-one; for a man, forty-eight. In 1950, the life expectancy for a woman had risen to seventy-two, and for a man to sixty-seven. Now there are about seventeen million people in the United States over sixty-five. It is estimated that there will be more than twenty million in 1975. Has science done us a favor in lengthening our life expectancy? Not necessarily, unless we learn to fill these added days with beauty, trust, usefulness, love. Someone commented, "We don't count the years until there is nothing else to count," and some facetious poet wrote:

> Of white hairs I surely have plenty,
> Of the years I have lived it's a proof,
> But while fire burns in the furnace,
> I don't mind all the snow on the roof!

Life is not a question of duration, but rather of intensity. All things being equal, those who live the longest are people who think the best thoughts, keep their minds stimulated with fresh ideas, and draw a vital fire from their inner spiritual resources that preserves their energies throughout the years. All too common today is the mistaken notion that to provide older folk with social security, a place to live, and plenty to eat is enough. But some of the loneliest people are those who draw the limit in social security, have a place to live, plenty to eat, and do a lot of traveling. Many a family thinks it is doing a great thing to find grandpa a nice retirement home where he can be with people "his own age." He may not want to be with people his own age. But he does want to be loved, needed, and useful. Life never finds its fulfillment in things, comforts. Life finds its fulfillment when one has discovered a philosophy to live by, and something to live for.

Throughout history some people have found the secret. Moses enlisted for his job at eighty, and of him it was said, "Moses was a hundred and twenty years old when he died; his eye was not dim, nor his natural force abated." Caleb had been promised a portion of the Promised Land when he was forty. He hadn't gotten it when he was eighty, but he went to Joshua and begged for his inheritance, not to be handed him on a silver platter. Caleb wanted a chance to fight for it. He said, "As yet I am as strong this day as I was in the day Moses sent me; as my strength was then, even so is my strength now, for war, both to go out, and to come in!"

John Wesley wrote in his journal on his seventy-first birthday, "I find just the same strength as I did thirty years ago . . . My sight is considerably better now, and my nerves firmer than they were then . . . I have none of the infirmities of old age, and have lost several I had in my youth." He attributed these blessings to the fact that for fifty years he got up at four o'clock in the morning for prayer and study, and that he traveled about 4,500 miles a year by horseback and coach helping people. George Mueller went to the mission field at sixty-five and worked for seventeen years, traveling and preaching in forty-two countries. Michelangelo was at his best at seventy, and some of Pasteur's best achievements came after he was sixty. Someone has estimated that sixty-four percent of the world's greatest achievements have been made by people past sixty—twenty-three percent by people between the ages of seventy and eighty, and thirteen percent by people under forty. So don't be too sure you can trust anyone under thirty. Better rethink that one.

It is not often that we find a person who seems to have really mastered later years. Occasionally there is one. Dr. E. Stanley Jones tells of a lady of 104 who was bright and spry. She had been a missionary to Burma. He found her reading aloud to herself from her Burmese Bible. She said, "I don't want to lose the accent." She probably felt she would need it in heaven to talk with her Burmese friends! One of my members at Trinity Methodist Church in Atlanta was a lady of indeterminate age. In one of my sermons I said something about growing old gracefully. After church she stopped on her way out the door and said, "I have no intention of growing old gracefully. I'm going to fight it every step of the way." She did, and what a contribution she made to countless lives!

Life ought to end "finished and fruitful" and not "frayed and frustrated." I would like to be able to come to the end of the way and say with Paul, "For I am already on the point of being sacrificed; the time of my departure has come. I have fought the good fight, I have finished the race, I have kept the faith. Henceforth there is laid up for me the crown of righteousness . . ." (II Timothy 4:6-8, RSV). Life makes demands of us, and as long as we meet them we never grow old. Growing old is a contradiction. We get old when we stop growing!

What then is the secret of the mastery of the later years in life?

1. Never stop learning. John Locke said, "It is a duty we owe to God to have our minds constantly open to receive and entertain new truth when we meet it." Our bodies sag because our minds are already sagging. Some boys asked an old man how he could be so spry and happy and radiant. He thought a moment, then pointed to a nearby apple tree in full bloom. He said, "Each year that apple tree grows a little new wood. When it stops it dies. Each year I try to grow a little new wood!"

There is nothing wrong with having a neck like a turkey as long as you don't have a mind like one. It is a fallacy that a person cannot learn in later years. We take it for granted that memory fails us and we can't do anything about it. An old lady said, "There are three things I can't remember: I can't remember names, I can't remember faces, and I . . . can't remember the third thing I can't remember." On the other hand John Wesley rode and read on horseback most of his life, and when he was too old to ride horseback, he had the inside of his carriage fitted with book shelves so that he could continue his study.

A wise professor told the graduates in one of our colleges, "If you young men will devote four hours a day to uninterrupted study, you'll never reach the deadline!" Better four hours of study than four hours before the "idiot box." Read books or have them read to you. Take advantage of lectures and of the short courses offered by most colleges. There is a wealth of opportunity to go on learning and growing mentally. You don't have to vegetate. Luther Burbank in *Harvest of the Years* wrote that he could never pass a strange plant, or see a carpenter using a new tool without asking, "What is this?" "I'm almost seventy-seven but I'm as inquisitive as I was at eight." [1]

2. *Keep up with the times.* How we hate change, especially as we get older. Our favorite pastime is to say "I remember when . . ." Memories are wonderful, but they are merely the frosting on the cake and not the cake. No one wants a steady diet of "I remember whens." It is foolish to stake out permanent residence at any given

---

[1] Luther Burbank, *Harvest of the Years* (Boston and New York: Houghton Mifflin Co., 1927).

point in our thinking or career. Everything changes. Change makes development possible. A salesman approached a farmer about buying a tractor. The farmer wouldn't hear of it. "For forty years I have been studying the tastes, the likes and dislikes of the mule, and I am not going to give up all that knowledge for any new-fangled tractor!"

Life is boring unless we keep up with the times. Oh, I don't mean that we should adopt every new fad that comes along, but act your age and keep up with the times. Know what is happening in the world. Have some opinions. Make decisions.

3. *Keep busy.* Don't overwork, but keep busy at something you like to do—something that is creative and makes a worthwhile contribution. The reason that many people die right after retirement is that they don't have anything useful to occupy their time. I know that those under thirty want their chance, and must have it, but I think compulsory retirement at sixty-five regardless of health or ability is wrong. In fact, I don't think a man ought to retire as long as he can get out of bed in the morning and put on his pants without leaning on his wife! When we stand still, we stagnate. If your company makes you retire at sixty-five, be getting ready to go into something else. Take a new vocation; don't just quit! Thomas Drier in *Clinical Medicine* magazine wrote, "The reason so many retired men die mentally is because they stop doing everything they do not want to do." Growth is the result of assuming obligations and taking responsibility. Retirement becomes a slow decay and death to many people.

It is important that we develop interests that will sustain us when retirement comes. Someone has spoken of "that other vocation," meaning the vocation of being Christian. We ought to build into life the compelling purpose of being evangelists for the Good News of the Christian faith. A seventy-one-year-old man called me recently and wanted me to go with him to visit another man the same age who had never made a profession of faith in Christ and had never joined the church. We were successful. What a vocation!

Every man has something to offer. It may be setting up a workshop in the basement and teaching neighborhood boys how to handle tools, something their fathers usually don't do. It may be substituting in the local schools for a sick teacher. It may be baby-sitting for a mother so she can go shopping. It may be a very simple thing, but the important thing is to keep busy.

4. Believe in yourself. It is fatal at any age to say, "I'm not worth anything to anybody—God or man!" Life has a worthwhile goal for each of us. We are made in God's image, and he needs us as long as we live. We may get rebellious because we can't see and taste and hear and digest as well as we once could, but adjust and go right on in the faith that God needs us. One of my favorite verses in the Bible is Mark 9:23: "If thou canst believe, all things are possible to him that believeth." One of my favorite poets is Edwin Markham. Remember his lines:

I am done with the years that were:
I am quits. I am done with the dead and the old.
They are mines worked out: I have delved in their pits,
I have saved their grains of gold.
Now I turn to the future for my bread and wine.
I have bidden the past adieu.
I laugh and lift my hands to the years ahead,
Come on! I'm ready for you.[2]

5. Live outside yourself. The tendency in later years is to get selfish and be concerned with only what concerns us. How desperately we need friends at this time! Charles

[2] Edwin Markham, *Poems of Edwin Markham*, selected by Charles L. Wallis (New York: Harper and Brothers, 1950).

Lamb once complained that all his friends, his school mates, his companions were gone. Samuel Johnson reminded him and us that "a man must keep his friendships in repair!" Friends are essential to happiness. We need people.

To have friends, we must be friendly and be interested in other people and what interests them. A man all wrapped up in himself makes a mighty small package. How many things there are that we can do in later years to cultivate people and live outside ourselves, get along with other people and be cheerful. Old age does not confer the right to be ornery or disagreeable, but neither does it confer wisdom. You can be just as stupid at seventy as at twenty.

Live outside of self. Visit friends in the hospital. Call friends on the telephone. Find out what is going on in the world and take a stand for the right thing. Encourage the young people you know. They may not trust anybody over thirty, but they need mature companionship. Cultivate them. Witness to your own love for Jesus at every opportunity. Not in an obnoxious way, but gently and with a prayer. Do all that you can for your church.

6. *Live close to God!* We need God all the time, but this is especially true in the final years of life. The person with a firm faith in God faces the later years of life eagerly and without fear. How important it is that we give ourselves to God early in life so that our companionship with him may deepen as the years go by! Several years ago I preached in an Older Adult Retreat at Reinhardt College. I told a story about a man coming to see me after being told he was going blind. The man was very agitated. Since he had been a member of the church for more than fifty years, I reminded him of the strengthening words in the Bible and of the fact that he could rely on the power of God for strength and help. But about the

saddest note I have ever heard came when he said, "I have no inner resource. I am not a Christian."

As soon as the service was over that day, one of the other men stopped to see me. He said that his doctor had told him the week before that he was going blind and there was no cure. But this man said, "Preacher, I'm not afraid. I have some inner resources. I am a Christian. I'll be all right!" What a contrast! It doesn't matter how much money you have, or what kind of a house, though these are important, but it does matter a great deal that you have inner resources, inner braces against the coming of the day when the physical man begins to fail and our senses are dimmed and dulled. We ought to be building up these resources by our growing trust in God so that we too may fulfill the prophecy, "At evening time it shall be light" (Zechariah 14:7).

Years ago, Dr. Walter Russell Bowie got a letter from a little boy. When the boy had said what he wanted to say, he concluded the letter by writing, "I hope you live all your life!" Toyohike Kagawa, the great Japanese Christian, prayed, "Though my muscles may stiffen, though my skin may wrinkle, may I never find myself yawning at life."

10

Your Home Has A Soul!

". . . and there he builded an altar unto the Lord."
Genesis 12:8
". . . and to the church in thy house . . ." Philemon 2

Robert Burns, the Scottish poet, was no saint, and yet
he had a tender feeling for the devotional practices of his
countrymen. His poem, "The Cotter's Saturday Night,"
describes a typical Saturday night in the home of a Scottish peasant. First, they sing:

> They chant their artless notes in simple guise,
> They tune their hearts, by far the noblest aim.

Then the father takes the Bible and reads from it:

> The priest-like father reads the sacred page,
> How Abram was the friend of God on high . . .
> Perhaps the Christian volume is the theme.
> How guiltless blood for guilty man was shed . . .

The singing and reading are followed by prayer:

> Then kneeling down to heaven's eternal King,
> The saint, the father, and the husband prays . . .

While reading this poem recently, a feeling of nostalgia came over me as I remembered my days as a boy on the farm, and later in the mill village. We took turns reading the Bible, and then we all knelt by our chairs for a time of prayer. We do it in a different way in our own home now, but the Bible and prayer are part of our way of life. I acknowledge that on those days when we do not quite make it for press of "more important things," I feel lonely and confused and things do not seem to go exactly right.

I am sure that to sophisticated, progressive, self-sufficient Americans this seems hopelessly old-fashioned and unnecessary. What is it that prayer can give us that we cannot get for ourselves? Anna Louis Strong went to Russia years ago and in the course of her interviews, she asked an old Russian peasant about the difference between old Russia and new Russia. He replied that in the old days, when the fields were plowed for sowing, the priest would come and lift his hands above them and bless them and pray that they would be fertile. But in new Russia, with improved fertilizer, new tractors, better seed, and new methods the priest isn't needed.

On the other hand the modern family may have all the gadgets and things science makes possible and still be unhappy and divided. Last year we Americans swallowed more than ten billion sleeping pills in an effort to find peace. And we took millions of aspirin to get relief from jangled nerves, and millions of gallons of whiskey were consumed to find escape from life's pressures. Maybe that old-fashioned Scottish family knew something that we have forgotten. Possibly we are missing something in our well-furnished, up-to-date houses that a very simple practice could give us.

The Bible joins together inseparably the home and religion. Long before Robert Burns, a man named Abraham left the place where he was born simply because he could no longer tolerate the wickedness. He set out, "not knowing whither he went," but everywhere he stopped with his family, he built an altar and worshiped God with his family. When Paul wrote his Philemon letter, he addressed it to "the church in thy house." Religion has its beginning in the family. The family finds its greatest strength in religion. Bishop Hazen G. Werner says "Religion and the family belong together. Here is history's greatest indentification. They complement each other, as the two blades of a pair of scissors." [1] This is what Horace Bushnell meant when he wrote, "Home and religion are kindred words; home, because it is the seat of religion; religion, because it is the sacred element of home. A house without a roof would scarcely be a more indifferent home than a family without religion." [2]

Many of the things that have happened to us in America have come because we have left God out of our families. A distinguished psychiatrist refers to ours as a "neurotic age." One of the acknowledged scandals of modern civilization, as well as one of the great perplexities to medical science, is the increasing number of ailments due to emotional disturbances. Fifty years ago we boasted that an increase in leisure time would make us healthier, happier people. That has been silenced by facts. We live longer. So what? We have not yet proven that we are happier. We are a nervous, hard-pressed, harried, defeated generation. Alexis Carrel said "that man simply does not have the nervous system to keep pace with modern civilization." A poet put it in simple lines:

> Said the robin to the sparrow
> I should really like to know
> Why these anxious human beings
> Rush about and worry so.

---

[1] Hazen G. Werner, *Christian Family Living* (1958), p. 19.

[2] Horace Bushnell, quoted by Hazen G. Werner, *Christian Family Living* (1958), p. 18.

> Said the sparrow to the robin,
> Friend, I think that it must be
> That they have no heavenly Father
> Such as cares for you and me.[3]

Though we do have a heavenly Father and God isn't dead, in far too many of our homes, our experience of him is dead.

The achievement of a Christian home is the family's most important function. I saw a sign recently that said "Home for Sale." You can't buy a home. Edgar A. Guest put it succinctly: "It takes a heap o' livin in a house t' make it home." [4] It sure does.

"Having a Christian home means far more than having a houseful of nice people who treat each other fairly well and who go to church fairly regularly. It means a home where Christ is known and loved and served, where children come to know him through their parents; where the Christian training of children is put ahead of the social ambition of the father; where the father is determined to carry on his business in conformity with the mind of Christ; where both father and mother are determined to make their social life conform to high Christian ideals; and where eyes see far horizons of a world to be won for Christ." [5] What a mighty definition of the Christian home. It is in a home like this that sound, Christian character is developed, genuine respect for each other is built up, and ideals are established that can never be dimmed.

---

[3] Quoted from "Your Home Has a Soul" by Bishop S. E. Garth, published by *Tidings*, General Board of Evangelism, The United Methodist Church, Nashville, Tenn.

[4] Edgar A. Guest, "Home," *Best Loved Poems of the American People* (Garden City: Garden City Publishing Company, 1936), p. 375.

[5] Paul S. Rees, *Christian: Commit Yourself* (Westwood, N.J.: Fleming H. Revell Co., 1947), p. 91.

We cannot keep our families together and happy and creative without God's help. Whom God hath joined together, God can keep together. It is in his strength that we achieve oneness and love comes to its fullest flower. It is in him that we find direction in every aspect of family living. John C. Wynn says, "Those parents whose Christian maturity has enabled them to find their way to God-in-Christ can possess a self-acceptance of a depth of understanding that is valued above mere techniques of child management, or even those newly popular skills of group relations." [6] Calvin Coolidge commented while president of the United States, "The greatest need of America is religion, the religion that centers in the home." And what he said then is very true today.

Not only is the achievement of a Christian home the family's most important function, it also is the family's greatest reward. We read that Abraham was "very rich in cattle, in silver, and in gold" (Genesis 13:2). I suspect if someone had said that to him, he would have pointed to the altar and said, "If I am rich, my friend, my real wealth lies around that altar you see there. It is God and my faith in him!"

This is what Karl J. P. Spitta meant when he wrote:

O happy home, where Thou art loved the dearest,
    Thou loving friend, and Saviour of our race,
And where among the guests there never cometh
    One who can hold such high and honored place!

O happy home, where two in heart united
    In holy faith and blessed hope are one,
Whom death a little while alone divideth,
    And cannot end the union here begun!

---

[6] John C. Wynn, "Questions for Key Parents," p. 8, Board of Christian Education, The Presbyterian Church in the U.S.A., 1957.

O happy home, where Thou are not forgotten
    When joy is overflowing, full, and free;
O happy home, where every wounded spirit
    Is brought, Physician, Comforter, to Thee—

Until at last, when earth's day's work is ended
    All meet Thee in the blessed home above,
From whence Thou camest, where Thou hast ascended,
    Thy everlasting home of peace and love! [7]

Happiness at home is closely tied in with religion at home. I honestly think the modern American family is beginning to wake up to the fact that salvation does not lie in better detergents, floor polishes, longer vacations, better housing. We have seen plenty of houses with all of these where there is no happiness. Happiness grows out of having some solid foundations, some sense of eternal values, some definite guidelines in discipline and purpose—not just a permissiveness that allows everything. Happiness, in short, grows out of a family's commitment to God and the things of God. Rather than detracting from fun and fulfillment, religion enhances and adds to these things. The Christian family can have more fun than any other.

In our preparation of couples for marriage, we spend some time emphasizing the importance of making the home Christian—a home where marriage partners are committed to God in Christ and where ample time is spent each day in devotional practices. I remember hearing a lecturer in college say that time spent by a husband and wife in prayer, Bible reading, and discussion of the things that really matter in life was much more intimate and wonderful than any sexual experience. The essential

---

[7] Karl J. P. Spitta, *Masterpiece of Religious Verse* (New York: Harper and Brothers, 1948), pp. 347, 348.

us cannot be satisfied with bread and drink and sex and money and things. The spirit must be fed also.

There are several things we can do to make our family practice of faith effective.

When you wake in the morning, breathe a prayer of thanksgiving to God for a new day with all its promise and possibility. It is his gift to us and we ought to dedicate it to him. Breathe a prayer for strength, courage, direction—a prayer that the day may not pass uselessly away. Utter a prayer that the day may be used for good for God and man, and dedicate it to the glory of God. Give thanks for physical strength, mental alertness, spiritual guidance.

Say something pleasant to the first person you meet. It will likely be either your husband or wife. The first time you do it, you may send him (her) into a state of shock. Many people go into the day grouchy and irritable simply because there is no discipline. It is not easy to say something happy and kind when you are half asleep, but the day will go better if you begin by saying, "I love you," or a pleasant "good morning."

Get up five minutes earlier if need be to have grace at the table and a time of Bible reading and prayer after breakfast. This will be the best time investment you can make. Let all the members of the family take part in turn, reading the Bible, leading the prayer, reading the meditation. Stress the importance of returning thanks at the table. This reminds us that we are not independent, that we didn't create it all, but that "every good and perfect gift is from above, and cometh down from the Father of lights, with whom is no variableness, neither shadow of turning" (James 1:17). Let meal time be a happy time, without quarreling, and certainly not a time to discipline anyone. It should be a time to recall the happy events of the day, or to make useful plans for the hours ahead. Meal time ought to be the happiest time of all for the entire family. Plan as many meals together as possible. Eating together as a family should be as much a sacrament as the Sacrament of the Lord's Supper—a sacred fellowship.

Fill "the chinks of time," as Dr. Frank Laubach calls them, with prayer. That is, don't just waste the time you ride along in a cab or on the bus, or the time you wait for your wife (or husband). I have a friend who carries a little book with him everywhere he goes. When he must wait for a red light, he reads a sentence or two. When an appointment is late, he absorbs the printed word. No wonder he is one of the most successful men I have ever known.

Some families have their main devotional period at night before retiring. The time doesn't matter. The fact that it is done is what counts. Collect a library of materials for use in daily devotions no matter when you have them. Several translations of the Bible, a good Bible story book, your denominational devotional booklet are all helpful. At times you may want to include selections from the great Christian classics. Actually, reading together in the family devotional period can help develop a love for good reading and fine books that will last a lifetime.

All members of the family should be regular attendants of the same church. Do more than "send" the children to Sunday school; take them. Support the church enthusiastically. Be active workers in the church up to the limit of your ability. Renewal will come when families renew their loyalty to the church—stop kicking and start supporting. A family at Sunday dinner was complaining about everything at church. The choir was sour, the sermon was too long, the seats were hard, and the sanctuary was too hot. Finally, little Bobby, who had seen what happened at church and heard what was said at home, got everybody's attention and said, "But Daddy, don't you think it was a pretty good show for a nickel?"

Finally, call your pastor when there is genuine need and he can be of help. I saw a bulletin recently that said, "Your pastor is as near as the telephone." Don't worry the daylights out of him with little things that don't matter, but don't hesitate to call him when you really need him. Let him in on your successes as well as your heartaches. He likes the bright side once in a while, too! Let him be a friend to the family. As Dr. Pierce Harris used to say, "Every time I pass a church, I stop and pay a visit, so at last when I'm carried in, they won't say 'Who is it?'" Make friends with your pastor and let him be a friend to the family, and when need comes, neither of you will be embarrassed!

You see, religion and the family go together. The family needs religion. Religion needs the family. Jesus turned to the family for his highest descriptions: God is Father; his own relationship to God was Son; members of the family of God are brothers and sisters; home is the word used for heaven; love is the chief characteristic of the Kingdom of God. After nearly twenty-five years of dealing with the family, I am more convinced than ever that without a vital Christian faith, the family has little chance of survival. Oh, it may survive, but it won't ever be the heaven on earth that it ought to be.

This story illustrates what I mean. A young woman came to her pastor for an interview. She was worried and said that her marriage was about to go on the rocks. The minister gathered that it was largely the husband's fault. Her husband was given to violent fits of temper and profanity. He must have been a very irritable man with whom to live. But there are always two sides to every problem, so he suggested that perhaps she had some responsibility for the situation. The minister then got to the point: Is there any religious atmosphere at all in the home? She admitted that there was not, "My husband talks about God a great deal, but not in the way you mean."

The minister outlined a way for her to begin a prayer life with her husband. He suggested that they begin by returning thanks at the table.

That night at dinner she said softly, "Jim, I sort of feel like I would like to return thanks, do you mind?" Astonishment spread over his features but he said nothing. Finally after several days of this at every meal, Jim growled, "Who is the head of this house anyway? I am going to return thanks myself." Presently, it got so they were discussing their problems and praying about them, and the atmosphere of the home changed until there was a reverence and a love about it.

"Happy the home when God is there!"

11

⚔⚔⚔⚔⚔⚔⚔

And Now You Live
Dispersed On Ribbon Roads

". . . lay up these words of mine . . . teach them to your children . . . that your days . . . may be multiplied . . ." Deuteronomy 11:18–21, RSV

Keith Miller, in his book, *A Second Touch*, tells of a man named Jack, an active churchman who was contemplating suicide. He had been successful "but he hated the person he had become." As a result of a new relationship with some people for whom religion was real and vital, Jack decided to give his future to God a day at a time. His wife made the same decision. Later, their twelve-year-old son came to talk with his father. The boy was in trouble at school, had no friends, and was very unhappy. He had seen a change in his dad, and came to ask him about it. The father said, "Well, son, I was making a big mess out of my life and I decided I'd ask God to take it over and show me how to live it." The boy thought a moment and then he said, "Dad, I think I'd like to do that too." Shortly thereafter the father went away on a business trip. When he returned after two weeks, his son met him at the airport and greeted him

breathlessly, "Daddy, do you know what God has done?"
"No, what son?" his dad asked. "He's changed every kid
in my class!" [1]

This book began with the insistence that everything
rises and falls with the home. Any community is but the
extension of the families that make it up.

The purpose of the family is to be a small community of
individuals where the secret of cooperative living is
learned and where personality has an opportunity for
fulfillment. But, the family must not be just a closely knit
unit—enjoying its own fellowship, thriving on its love for
each other, living for itself. Like a pool into which water
flows, but from which there are no outlets, the self-satis-
fied family becomes stagnant and stale. The family must
move out into the community and the world to be Christ's
instrument in a reconciling, healing, saving ministry.
Home is the beginning point for such things as honesty,
respect for law and order, world peace, respect for human
personality—one's own, as well as that of others. It is the
place where one learns that his body is the temple of the
Holy Spirit. These virtues must find application in all the
relationships of a family with the world. The family must
become a moving force in the community to transform all
that is ugly, blighted, hateful, sinful into that which is
beautiful, alive, loving, right. Someone has said that while
a setting can make a diamond, a genuine diamond can
transform any old setting. A community influences the
family, but the opposite is also true: the family ought to
transform the community.

Joanna C. Colcord has described the meaning of family:
"The individual must have somewhere a group who cares
about what happens to him; and this caring must be more
vital than the loose and casual interest of a group of

---

[1] Keith Miller, *The Second Touch* (Waco, Texas: Word
Books, Publisher, 1967).

friends or a fraternal organization. The life of this group must be so bound up with the individual that it is a matter of the deepest importance to them what he does or becomes." [2] This is true. It is this lack of "we-ness" that lies at the root of many of our problems. T. S. Eliot has put it poignantly in one of his choruses from a favorite poem of mine entitled, "The Rock":

> What life have you if you have not life together?
> There is no life that is not in community,
> And no community not lived in praise of God.
> Even the anchorite who meditates alone,
> For whom the days and nights repeat the praise of God,
> Prays for the church, the Body of Christ incarnate.
>
> And now you live dispersed on ribbon roads,
> And no man knows or cares who is his neighbor
> Unless his neighbor makes too much disturbance,
> But all dash to and fro in motor cars,
> Familiar with the roads and settled nowhere.
> But every son must have his own motor cycle
> And daughters ride away on casual pillions.[3]

Fortunate are the children whose parents can give them a basic, ineradicable sense of belonging which inoculates them against the ravages of the destructive economic and social forces of the age. But, such a wonderful family relationship must be the launching pad from which the family takes off to be a redemptive, wholesome, transforming influence on the community, the nation, and the world. Every facet of the community must feel the impact of the Christian family. The final test of the worth,

---

[2] Joanna C. Colcord, *Social Forces*, 6:577–579, June, 1928.

[3] T. S. Eliot, "Choruses from the Rock, *The Complete Poems and Essays* (New York: Harcourt, Brace and Company, 1952), p. 101.

stability, and faith of the family is found in the way it discharges its responsibilities to society as an uplifting, saving force. What Jesus said of the individual and final greatness applies to the family as well: "For I was an hungered, and ye gave me meat: I was thirsty, and ye gave me drink: I was a stranger, and ye took me in: Naked, and ye clothed me: I was sick, and ye visited me: I was in prison, and ye came unto me . . . Inasmuch as ye have done it unto one of the least of these my brethren, ye have done it unto me" (Matthew 25:35–40).

Out there are a sick world, sick cities, sick churches, sick business—naked, hungry, and enslaved people. The final test of the worth of the family is in what it does with the wonderful unity and the beautiful relationships enjoyed with each other.

Take renewal in the church, for example. It may begin in the individual family that takes religion seriously and becomes intimately involved in the life of the church. Whenever a family decides to give itself wholly to God with no strings attached and become deeply involved in the prayer life of the church, the witness of the church to the world, the missionary outreach of the church, the tithing program, the program of Christian education, it can be the nucleus of a startling renewal in the vigorous life of the church. The church is not made strong by the number on the rolls, but it is strong in direct proportion to the number of members who assume responsibility for being full-time Christians in all the relationships of life.

I believe there is a need for Christians to assume some responsibility for the entertainment world. Someone was telling me recently of attending a new dinner theater. She had called the management in advance to find out what kind of play was being given and was assured that it was "family" entertainment. The play had just started when she realized that she had made a terrible mistake. There was a variety of four and five letter words. Sex was raw, and the young people present in the theater sat spellbound as the action built up to the act of adultery. The action stopped with a bedroom door closing on two people whose intentions were unmistakable.

My friend looked around to see if anyone was present who knew her. But she said her real concern was for the young people who were there. Where were their parents? At home, perhaps, watching television, thinking their children were safe in some little dinner theater where they couldn't get into trouble. Someone has said, "Some families can trace their ancestry back three hundred years, but can't tell you where their children were last night."

How long has it been since you protested indecent films? How long since any protest came from your house on violence, drinking, sex perversion in the shows on television? Recently, I passed a theater where a highly touted film was showing. It was supposed to reveal the facts of life, down to the minutest detail. The ad read, "No one under 16 admitted." I stood and watched the ticket sales a moment. Business was brisk. Many were even under twelve. I went inside and protested to the manager, and he told me to "mind my own business." A report to authorities got no response. Movie censorship is out. Possibly there are no rigid laws, but the one law such people respond to is the click of the turnstile. The family ought to know what is going on and say "No!" and mean it. We would be fighting mad if the service station attendant poured impure gas into our automobile tanks— we love our cars. We would be furious if the grocer sold us impure food, or if the druggist sold us impure drugs— we love our bodies. And yet, we let our children poison their souls with impure movies, television, and comic books. Someone has said,

Vice is a monster of so frightful mien,
As to be hated, needs but to be seen;
Yet seen so oft, familiar with her face,
We first endure, then pity, then embrace.

Here is another example of Christian opportunity and responsibility. Dr. Lee H. Bristol, Jr., tells of a businessman standing in New York's Penn Station one day, when an unshaven man walked up to him and said, "You look friendly," and then told him a sad story of a wasted life. When he finished, he asked, "Will you do something for me? You know, there's not a soul in the world who cares if I live or die. Would you mind thinking about me for a couple of weeks? If I could think there was someone somewhere thinking about me as a human being, it would be worth a million dollars to me." The man slipped into the crowd, nameless.

The family must become concerned with persons. It is in the family that we teach respect for people, all people. Our prejudices against people are learned. They are not hereditary. Jokes about other races, names like "nigger," "wop," "dago," "whitey," and the insinuation that we are better than others make an impression on children and often create a prejudice that lasts a lifetime.

It is not enough merely to teach the truth that God is the Father of all mankind and that all men are brothers; this fundamental doctrine must be practiced by the family in its relationship to men of other races, men who live in slums, men who are poverty-stricken, and people who are victims of alcoholism and dope addiction. We must see them as men for whom Christ died and for whom love and healing are available. "Him that cometh to me I will in no wise cast out," said Jesus (John 6:37). This means everybody. The family must lend its efforts to every means to eliminate racial discrimination against black and white—to eliminate poverty by helping those who cannot help themselves and by helping those who can help themselves; by eliminating slums and teaching people how to live in houses and make homes of them; by seeing that all men get as much education as they can usefully receive; and by seeing that everyone has an opportunity to use his abilities in full service of God and man.

Freedom with responsibility for all men must become the goal of the Christian family. But every man must be seen as divinely made, divinely endowed, and given divine responsibilities to perform. The family must work for the enactment of laws that will fulfill the deepest intent of the Constitution, the Bible, and basic human rights. In short, we must demonstrate to the community that "someone somewhere is thinking about" other people and working for their fulfillment.

So few families get involved in the educational process of their children. Yet, when a child fails, we always blame the schools. Encourage parents to join the Parents and Teachers Association. Here is one of the cherished institutions of society, and yet the family often stands aside and leaves the education of children to "those trained for it." Ideally, school and family form a partnership. It is a rare thing that miracles happen in education unless there is some encouragement at home. A teacher came to Johnny's house and told his mother that the boy just was not cooperating at school. When the teacher left, the mother asked for an explanation. "Well, it's like this," Johnny said, "she just doesn't teach anything that I want to learn."

Education is a strange combination of facts from books, attitudes toward life, a philosophy to live by, and a direction to go by. Book learning is not enough. Character learning is also a part, and it is at this point that home makes its best contribution to the whole process of education. But, unfortunately, too many parents let their children grow as they will and study if they want to without much conscious effort or cooperation on their part. *School Management* had an incisive paragraph in it years ago: "The trouble with the school system today is, the teachers are afraid of the principals, the principals are afraid of the superintendent, he is afraid of the school committee, they are afraid of the parents, the parents are afraid of their children, and the children are afraid of nobody." The family must be involved in education if education is to be preparation for total living. The Supreme Court decision outlawing compulsory prayer and Bible reading in public schools has done us one service: it placed character education in the lap of the family.

Take one more illustration. A sense of patriotism for our country must be taught in the family. It is corny to be patriotic today, and maybe I am a flag waver, but as Dr. R. Harvey Bodine has said, ". . . before one gives up waving the flag of our country, one ought to be certain he has a better flag to wave; for everyone waves some flag." [4] There is now a strange attitude toward patriotism. A survey was made of high school students visiting the Hall of Free Enterprise at the World's Fair in New York. It showed that forty percent could name no advantage democracy has over communism; sixty percent thought the government ought to take over most of the nation's industries; and eighty-four percent felt that patriotism is unnecessary. What has happened to the feeling of loyalty for our country? I listened recently as a man lambasted the United States roundly for Viet Nam, bad domestic policy, too much spending, etc., etc., etc. When he was through, I asked, "How would you like to live in East Berlin, or South America?" He was thoughtful for a mo-

---

[4] R. Harvey Bodine, *Best Sermons*, edited by Paul G. Butler (New York: Trident Press, 1966–68), vol. x, p. 287.

ment and then replied, "You know, I hadn't thought of that." Howard Whitman once wrote in *This Week:*

> Is mature love of country blind and uncritical? Take Stephen Decatur's famous line: "Our country! . . . May she always be right, but our country, right or wrong!" How shall we interpret it? "Well, it's like this," said one of my neighbors. "It's like the way I feel about my son. Naturally I want him to go straight. But if he doesn't go straight, sure—I'll still love him. I'll love him in a sad kind of way. I'll tell him, 'Look Butch, you're wrong.' I'll work hard every single minute to try to make him go straight. . . . Our country right or wrong—but we have to work all the time to make it right!"

Our attitude toward our country should be that of a wife to her husband. A loving wife will do almost anything for the man she loves except stop trying to improve him. And we should cast affectionate, if at times, sharp glances, toward our country. True, there are things wrong with it that must be corrected. But these are not corrected by teaching our children to hate the President, curse the Supreme Court, vilify the Governor, burn draft cards, demonstrate, riot, destroy, kill. Every effort must be made to change what is wrong in the nation, but changes ought to take place through the channels now provided for that purpose: court, legislature, ballot box. Peter wrote, "Submit yourselves to every ordinance of man for the Lord's sake: whether it be to the king, as supreme; or unto governors, as unto them that are sent by him for the punishment of evil doers, and for the praise of them that do well" (I Peter 2:13–14). While working for peace in the world, for the best government possible, for the rectification of every wrong, whether racial or economic, I must remain patriotic, teach my children the basic history of the United States, and lead them to a love for country and a pride in the possibilities of our nation.

Henry Drummond put it well when he said, "The final test of religion is not religiousness, but love—not what I have done, not what I have believed, not what I have achieved, but how I have discharged the common charities of life." So with the family. The final test of the worth of the family lies in its impact on community, nation, school, church, government, world. Our homes must become the launching pad from which we move into every area of human life and to be what Jesus meant when he said, "Ye are the light of the world. A city that is set on a hill cannot be hid" (Matthew 5:14). Good family life is the nation's most priceless asset. Dr. Robert A. Raines tells of a woman who works as a secretary. She commented on a particular issue to her boss. He said to her, "Did you get that idea from the funny little church you go to?" At first she was irritated, but when she regained her composure she replied, "I'm glad my funny little church shows." [5] These funny "little homes" of ours show, too. What impact does ours have on the community where we live? On the place where we work? . . . on the school our children attend? . . . and on the country that we love? Do they show in relationship to the needs of men, whatever they are and wherever they live?

I have a friend who has four children, ranging from elementary school to college. They seem to have a genuine concern for other people—not only for each other, but for neighbors nearby and throughout the world. I asked him one day how he and his wife had been so successful with their family. He said, I think facetiously, "Only by the grace of God," but he hit upon a great truth. No family can accomplish their goals without the grace of God in abundance.

---

[5] Robert A. Raines, *New Life in the Church* (New York: Harper and Brothers, 1961), p. 131.

For Further Reading

A Slow and Certain Light. *Elisabeth Elliot.*

Do you really know what God's will is for you and your life? How does your own self-will fit into this master plan? A collection of observations from Elisabeth Elliot's personal experience and from the Bible on why and how God does, in fact, guide his children. #80318 (hardback).

Prayer Power. *J. Moulton Thomas.*

Here is a handbook for informal prayer in small groups—a helpful tool to bridge the gap between individual prayer and corporate prayer. Helpful guidelines are offered for getting through obstacles— inadequate time, idols, self-pity, overconscious effort, resentment, and guilt—so that prayer can become honest sharing and a vital part of the Christian's commitment. #98066 (paperback).

Peace with the Restless Me. *Janice W. Hearn.*

How Christians can overcome depression and bitterness in their lives. In this real-life pilgrimage from futility to fulfillment, Mrs. Hearn shares what she is learning about love, joy, peace, patience, kindness, generosity, fidelity, adaptability, and self-control . . . how the Holy Spirit transforms the believer's attitudes by working from the inside out. #80455 (hardback).

How Come We're Alive? *Curtis Jones.*

This book will help you see life's heartaches—fear, loneliness, suffering—in proper perspective. Dr. Jones brings together real-life experiences, anecdotes, and incidents from history and literature to show that the negative things of life can be redemptive if we will allow God to mold our character through them. #98067 (paperback).

Prayers from Where You Are. *Francis A. Martin.*

A sensitive collection of prayers from the heart. They are personal, yet they speak a universal language because they come from deep within the soul. Each prayer has a spontaneity about it that makes it fresh and relevant for today. #98035 (paperback).

Bread for the Wilderness/Wine for the Journey. *John Killinger.*

Out of his own pilgrimage, John Killinger shares with us the deeper meaning of prayer and the inner life, and his own growing conviction that prayer is real. He helps us learn to be more attuned to the things of the spirit and the mystery of God's leading. #80443 (hardback).

All You Lonely People/All You Lovely People. *John Killinger.*

Who of us dares to admit our loneliness? John Killinger found the courage to share himself and his loneliness in a small caring group to which he and his wife belonged for a few months. A look at how a small group can become the body of Christ—with life-changing results. #80315 (hardback).

Search for Silence. *Elizabeth O'Connor.*

A marvelous book for helping us get in touch with our real self—that inner reality we so often neglect, ignore, or push away. With realism, Miss O'Connor helps us face our two-sidedness, and then calls us to prayer and contemplation—and to action. Excerpts from other authors provide further material for reflection and meditation. #80264 (hardback).

Eighth Day of Creation. *Elizabeth O'Connor.*

After we have accepted ourselves, and have found that place where we can hear God speak to us, then we are called upon to act. God himself calls us to join the creative forces in the world by discovering our own creativity and gifts. Knowing who we are means that we acknowledge what it is our gift to do. Excerpts from other authors provide material for meditation. #80260 (hardback).

Dare to Be You. *James R. Dolby.*

An adventure in self-discovery, *Dare to Be You* is a springboard for fresh thinking and lively discussion in various areas of religious experience and daily life. The section "As the Twig Is Bent" traces the emotional and spiritual growth of the child from birth through the college years. #91005 (Key-Word paperback).

Yes Is a World. *James W. Angell.*

A rousing welcome into the life of affirmation. This hope-filled book includes chapters titled: Man Is Born with Rainbows in His Heart; Not the Postponed Life;

Transcendence Is a Kiss on the Nose; Instructions for
Erecting a Tent in a Rainstorm; Yes Got Up Before
the Sun; Dancing on a Battlefield. #80387 (hardback).

The Gift of Wholeness. *Hal L. Edwards.*
The warmly human story of a modern pilgrim in
search of himself . . . and in search of God. A refreshing look at one minister and his ministry—a
vulnerable, open kind of life that grows and keeps on
growing. #80377 (hardback).

Barefoot Days of the Soul. *Maxie D. Dunnam.*
Remember when you were a child how you longed
for the first warm days of spring when your mother
finally let you go barefoot? How marvelous and free
it felt. "Nothing in my experience," says Maxie Dunnam, "is more suggestive of the promise of the gospel
than that. This book is about freedom. It's a thank-you
celebration—an invitation to barefoot days of the
soul." #80432 (hardback).

The One and Only You. *Bruce Larson.*
People don't come in carbon copies. We may accept
that idea, but how do we make the most of being one
of a kind? Bruce Larson is convinced that every one
of us unique "yous" has an unlimited potential to
draw on—the liberating security of God's love. Here
he probes what that can mean for us and gives us
practical ways of putting our potential to work.
#91012 (A Key-Word paperback).

Let God Love You. *Lloyd John Ogilvie.*

In thirty-eight devotional meditations, the author takes the struggles of life seriously and turns them into stepping stones to Christian growth. Paul's letter to the Philippians forms the basis for these refreshing thoughts. #80353 (hardback).

The Becomers. *Keith Miller.*

A helpful and insightful look at what happens to a person after he or she becomes a Christian. Realistic, honest, and full of hope, for people who "are in the process of becoming whole as we reach out with open and creative hands toward work, people, and God." #80321 (hardback).

Habitation of Dragons. *Keith Miller.*

"Miller is forceful, witty, honest and surprising in his interpretation of a Christian life style. [Here] we have a combat diary for people trying to enlarge on the spiritual dimensions of existence"—David Poling, *New York Times.* Divided into forty-two selections, *Habitation of Dragons* is a book to be lived with one day at a time. #80182 (hardback). #91010 (a Key-Word book).

Come to the Party. *Karl A. Olsson.*

An invitation to a celebration of life. God invites us to his party, but some of us are like the older brother —we look on from the outside, knowing the party is not for us—we are not free to accept the love and blessing of our Father. Learn with Karl Olsson how to enter into a freer life style, secure in the love of God. #80296 (hardback). #98001 (paperback).

Enjoy the Journey. *Lionel A. Whiston.*

Accepting the fact that God loves us in spite of our failures, understanding our fellow man, and facing up to moral responsibility are just a few of the keys to a fuller spiritual life which Lee Whiston discusses in his warm and personal way in this helpful book. #80250 (hardback).